An Island in Time

NH

ATLANTIC

Boston

MA

CT RI

Cape Cod

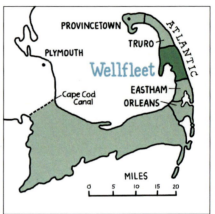

PROVINCETOWN

TRURO

PLYMOUTH

Wellfleet

ATLANTIC

Cape Cod Canal

EASTHAM

ORLEANS

MILES

0   5   10   15   20

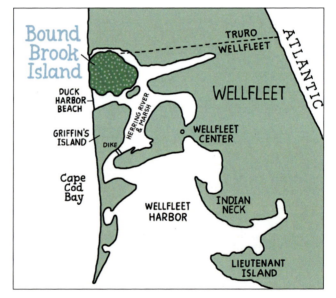

Bound Brook Island

TRURO
WELLFLEET

ATLANTIC

DUCK HARBOR BEACH

WELLFLEET

HERRING RIVER & MARSH

GRIFFIN'S ISLAND

DIKE

WELLFLEET CENTER

Cape Cod Bay

WELLFLEET HARBOR

INDIAN NECK

LIEUTENANT ISLAND

An Island in Time

Exploring Bound Brook Island
Its Land & People, Its Past & Present

Sharon Dunn

The Rose Press
LEVERETT, MASSACHUSETTS

For information about reproducing selections from
this book, email sharonrosedunn@gmail.com

An Island in Time incorporates memoir and historical research. I focused on the
parts of Bound Brook Island's story that fascinated me, so this is by no means a complete
history, but rather a selective and suggestive one. The individuals and events are real.
Their treatment is imaginative and based on the facts I could find.

The following poems in *An Island in Time* appeared in the *Cape Cod Poetry Review*
in summer 2021: "Island Road," "The Bunting Family Leaves," "Blackfish,"
"Bound Brook Camp Meetings, 1823–5," "Etched," "Lament,"
"The Borning Room in the Ebenezer L. Atwood House,"
"The Walk I Take to Fall Asleep at Night," and "The Old One."

Editing by Jean Zimmer
Book design by Greta D. Sibley
Author's maps rendered by Stephanie Peterson Jones

Painting on page xiv: Ebenezer L. Atwood House by Laura Clayton Baker

Printed in the United States of America
(ISBN: 978-1-951928-47-6)

Published by The Rose Press
Leverett, Massachusetts

For John J. Clayton

What makes a place special is the way it buries itself
inside the heart. . . .

—*Richard K. Nelson*

Knowing the past will be Cape Codders' best preparation
for their sublime, unpredictable future.

—*John R. Gillis*

Contents

Acknowledgments

THANK YOU TO CORINNE DEMAS AND MATTHEW ROEHRIG, who brought us to Bound Brook Island the very first time and to Joan Hopkins Coughlin for many hours of conversation about the island. I thank Cape Cod National Seashore Park Historian William Burke for encouragement and access to archives at the Salt Pond Visitor Center in Eastham, and I also thank the Wellfleet Historical Society. For assistance in my Lorenzo Dow Baker research, I thank Rebekah Ambrose-Dalton, archivist at the William Brewster Nickerson Cape Cod History Archives at Cape Cod Community College. Appreciation to Michael Parlante for bushwhacking for cellar holes with me, and love to these Bound Brook Island families: Hall, Taylor, Williams, Biddle, Levin, Fredricksen, and Miller. Deep gratitude to Martha Collins for her reading and suggestions. For their inspiration, I thank writers Robert Finch for rendering Cape Cod, present and past, and John Hanson Mitchell for his *Ceremonial Time*.

Prologue

HOW FATEFUL THE HANDSHAKE on the driveway thick with oyster shells—
Jack Hall holding out his big, speckled hand to me. We set off on foot together
across the sandy seventeenth-century cart road and through the cut in the wild
hedge. There it was: broad lawn, gnarled mulberry tree spreading shade, and
an old Cape house, the only one for sale on Wellfleet's Bound Brook Island in
decades.

So began our summers on Bound Brook Island, in northwestern Wellfleet
on Cape Cod, Massachusetts, my husband and I deciding this weathered, almost 200-year-old Cape house was meant to be ours—ours, but not exactly a
possession, a home in our safekeeping. John, a writer and academic, had summers to himself—and I could craft my own work arrangement in my family
business. So began my explorations of this piece of earth, with Jack Hall as
my mentor—Jack, tall and craggy, who had lived on Bound Brook for over 50
years, since his twenties, and who took me on hike after hike, passing along
stories and his love for this quiet place and what he knew of its history.

It didn't occur to me at the time that our decision to make Bound Brook
Island part of our lives would offer me an experience of place that would light

my imagination and curiosity. But the island held secrets of the past in the quiet of the present. For example, why was it called an island, when it clearly was not? I began writing poems about it. It was like falling in love—I wanted to know everything about the object of my love.

Soon I was delving into the island's geology, ecology, and archaeology, its maritime and salt industries, its religious camp meetings, the coming of the railroad, the diking of a river. I was meeting long-gone sea captains, entrepreneurs, a preacher, a midwife, and women who spun, gardened, cooked, and bore child after child. And, in the twentieth century, I encountered artists and intellectuals. I used US Censuses, archived newspapers, Barnstable County deeds and wills, and handwritten town meeting notes from Wellfleet and Truro to learn about the island's inhabitants and their lives; I pored over antique maps with a magnifying glass; I hunted down old photographs and took my own.

———

Less than three hours: That is how long it takes to walk around the base of the hilly landform that is Bound Brook Island. Its area is approximately one square mile. In your circuit on the edges of the island you'd be slowed by the narrowness and roughness of the footpath in some places. In others, the lush overgrowth of the last century—large trees and roots, thick shrubs—would stymie your way forward and force you to weave around. Some traipsing would be required on damp terrain because the robust river and brook waters of the past are now mainly marshland. Walking would be easy on the west perimeter, however, less than half a mile on a sandy beach.

———

My twenty-first century rendering of Bound Brook Island is personal, blending my observations and perceptions with facts and stories I researched and gathered as my curiosity and love deepened. I want the island to remain the haven I've found it to be, a quiet place where one can begin to apprehend what the old days felt like—no tarred roads, no noise from Route 6, no cell

"SLOW! Dogs . . . Children . . . Walkers"

service, no store, and most houses hidden from view by vegetation gone wild. Signs are few; my favorite is Jack's daughter Noa's, scripted in red paint on rough board nailed to a tree by the sandy road.

ISLAND ROAD

Moccasins and bare feet tamped a path,
then settlers' carts widened the trail.
Down what is now a sandy road,
grass growing in the middle,
a car drives slowly, scratched by arcs
of thorny rose, beach plum, scrub oak,
the road so narrow a newcomer wonders
Is a car allowed, am I trespassing?

This quiet morning the tawny sand
is pressed with pawprints, footprints,
zigzag tire treads, tracks of mouse,
rabbit, deer. Here, a half mile from the Bay,
lavender oyster shells and thick shards
of ancient clamshell emerge from the sand.
A walker's piled shells and chunks of brick
atop the grassy road bank, a cache of the past,
chimney brick from a house moved
off-island long ago.
                    The road, mottled
gold in sun, purple in shade, descends,
follows the curve of a ghost estuary
on its way west to the bay.

I

What It's Like Here

OFTEN I WALKED WITH MY DOG PRINCE down the two narrow, sandy roads of Bound Brook Island—yes, the island has but two roads. Our neighbors the Halls, Jack's family, always called them cart paths because carts traveled here first, before wagons, before cars.

Cart Paths, Forgotten Roads, and Footpaths

In a few places the banks of sandy Bound Brook Island Road rise to more than five feet, a testament to the hundreds of years the cart paths have been in use. Perhaps one of the paths will evolve into what author Robert Macfarlane has celebrated as a *holloway* in South Dorset, England, "a sunken path, a deep and shady lane . . . that centuries of foot-fall, hoof-hit, wheel-roll and rain-run have harrowed deep down," often with trees growing around and over, so that they are indeed "hole ways."

A single road brings you onto Bound Brook Island, from Wellfleet to the south or from Truro to the north. For the first thousand feet or so the road is paved, up to the entrance to the Atwood-Higgins property on the left, with its

1700s Cape house out of sight way down a hill and its replica rural structures built in the twentieth century. After this, Bound Brook Island Road is sand, and only one car at a time can pass along it. Coming in the opposite direction, another car must find a spot to lay by, and sometimes this takes considerable backing up. Roadside vegetation grows so lushly in places that it grazes the car. A second road, called Bound Brook Island Way, branches off to the northwest, following a ridge most of the way. That is the sum total of roads here.

Old roads—abandoned cart paths—lace Bound Brook Island. As I first walked the woods I came across indentations, almost trenches, sometimes several feet deep and entirely overgrown with grasses, often with mature trees growing in the middle. These forsaken cart roads lead to where families once lived and to the abundant salt marshes where they harvested hay as food and bedding for livestock.

I tracked one of these overgrown cart paths north from the Captain Baker (now Baker-Biddle) property. I climbed over fallen trees and through thickets of poison ivy to where the almost-hidden path joins today's Bound Brook Island Way. A hundred years ago five houses lay on either side of this forgotten way—they are dots on the old maps—but no visible traces remained as I traipsed along, swatting away biting blackflies. I walked a ghost road past ghost houses.

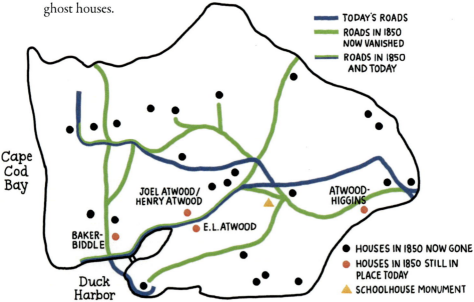

Twenty-three houses and many cart paths that existed in 1850 have disappeared from Bound Brook Island.

A centuries-old footpath in the northwest part of Bound Brook Island

Another old cart path, a favorite hiking trail today, runs east–west mostly on the highest ridge on the south side of the island. Bound Brook Island's many ghost roads show how connected the island was in the mid-1800s, when a larger community inhabited it. Now, like the community that once flourished here, these old cart paths have all but disappeared.

Slender footpaths abound on the island. Created by folk and by animals, mostly deer and fox, these traces may be just a line in the pine needles or a sinuous, sandy, six-inch-wide path amongst heather.

The Nameless Beach

In early morning I walk the beach on the western flank of Bound Brook Island, and often I cannot see a soul to my north or south. Somehow this bayside beach has remained nameless on all maps. Its sand is beige and rough grained, and its wrack lines are strewn with seashells, gull feathers, necklaces of seaweed, dark-brown husks of horseshoe crabs, and the occasional flotsam and jetsam of civilization—wood from a dock, a plastic water bottle, gift wrap ribbon, and sometimes a lobster buoy. The littoral—the zone between high and low tides—shows the prints of gulls, sandpipers, deer, dog paws, and our bare feet.

Over the centuries, the sands and sand dunes have come and gone. I find the remains of a beautiful gray cedar tree root, revealed only at low tide. Does this mean a cedar forest once thrived here? And are the barrier dunes at the end of Bound Brook Island Road new in the last 200 years? Are the dunes today lower than they were in the past? Did the Cape Cod Bay waters flow 300 feet closer to Captain Baker's house than they do now? There is no history of the sands, of where they have shifted, duned, or drifted away.

This beach constitutes the entire western shore of Bound Brook Island. The town of Plymouth lies 30 miles west, across Cape Cod Bay, to the left in this north-facing photograph.

At the southernmost access to the beach, five cars can manage to park in the small space that is, in places, deep sand, and cars routinely get stuck. Toting towels and books, we walk from our house down the sandy road for 10 minutes, pass the few parked cars, climb the dunes, and descend to the beach. We usually go at the end of the day—say, four o'clock—when the sun is less strong, and stay for about an hour. And sometimes we go at night to build a small fire and sit around it with friends.

Some years I walk over the dune when we arrive in late May and find much of the beach cobbled with rock. This makes walking into the water painful and unsteady, and I have to find a smoother place farther up or down the beach. I used to think the rocks had moved, but in fact they are always there, covered or not by the ever-migrating sands.

The dunes, beach, and shoreline change over time. In the early 1990s several sandbars appeared at low tide. I could sit on a sandbar with my young son and we could be on our own small island. Years later the bars disappeared. The dunes change too, mostly from winter storms. The dune path we took 20 years ago is no longer there, and we now climb a sister dune to the left to reach the beach.

There's a second beach access to the north where even fewer cars can park. These limitations are what keep folks away from Bound Brook's beach—driving for 10 minutes down a narrow sandy road, a ravine on each side, to find that you can't park your car is not vacation fun. Yet occasional walkers, swimmers, sun-lovers, and, every now and then, anglers enjoy the beach.

The very special time on our bay beach is sunset at low tide: The brilliant sun descends to the horizon and sinks into the sea, the glory of colors—purple, burnt orange, rose—playing in the panorama of clouds, mirrored on the water.

Schoolhouse Memorial and a Cellar Hole

Jack, in shorts, hiking boots, and plaid shirt, stopped short on one of our early walks: "Finally, here it is." He'd found a particular tree, his morning's quest, but he was tuckered out by the bushwhacking. He was, after all, almost 80 years old. We had been up and down the steep, small hills and ravines on Bound Brook Island all morning. He'd found the tree on a narrow trace at the base of a hill. Years ago he'd painted a picture of this oak, and then he'd forgotten where the tree was. We had been winding round a small pond turned wetland, a depression originally created by the weight of a chunk of glacier. And that oak tree: Well, you would pass it by—old, crooked, leaning. But when the tree was younger—and Jack was younger—he'd seen something worth capturing on canvas. "Where's that painting now?" I asked. "Oh, I gave it away a long time ago. I don't recall who to." Then we tramped back home to our houses, sited across from each other on the cart path.

Each time we set out, we had a new destination, I and this man old enough to be my father. (In fact, Jack was born in 1913, three years after my own father's birth and in the same city, New York.) One day we ambled up our sandy road and took a footpath off to the right through the woods. At the top of the broad hill amidst pitch pines stood a boulder four feet high, with a bronze plaque bolted on.

> **ERECTED**
>
> **IN**
>
> **GRATEFUL REMEMBRANCE**
>
> **OF**
>
> **THE ISLAND SCHOOL HOUSE**
>
> **1924.**
>
> **THOUGH FEW REMAIN WHO ONCE MET HERE**
> **AND SCATTERED ARE AFAR AND NEAR,**
> **WITH LOVE THEY HOLD IN MEMORY STILL,**
> **THE ISLAND SCHOOL HOUSE ON THE HILL**
> **AND GLADLY DO THEY MARK THE SPOT**
> **THAT IT MAY NEVER BE FORGOT.**

Carved into the rock below the plaque were the words "BUILT 1844."

Why was this modest memorial hidden in the middle of the woods? It sat 200 yards from the road and was not visible from it. Who decided to memorialize a beloved schoolhouse? Why was no brick or scrap of wood left to show where it once stood?

Only a community that had many families with young children would build a schoolhouse. Yet as I came to know the island at the end of the twentieth century, the Halls—Jack and his wife Mardi in their antique Cape—were the *only* year-round residents; the few other antique houses and twentieth-century houses were occupied only in summertime and at the edges of spring and autumn, owners closing them up for the rest of the year. I was beginning to wonder how many families once lived here, where and how they lived, and why they left.

Thrashing his way east of the schoolhouse memorial by about 50 steps, through a thicket of grasses and gnarly pitch pine branches, Jack led me to a cellar hole where, he told me, a house like mine had once stood. I saw scattered bricks, the deep hole, a hearthstone. Jack scanned the landscape: Over there, he spotted the stand of lilac where the outhouse would have stood. He told me that anywhere I saw a stand of lilac on the island meant that an outhouse once stood there.

"Aha! There's the mulberry tree that's the match for the one in your yard," he said, pointing toward a skeletal tree. Our huge spreading mulberry, about 100 years old, has been wired together; we had an arborist recommend how to "feed" it to keep it healthy, producing leaves and mulberries. "This tree's not doing so well, so many branches broken off," Jack said, shaking his head. However, he was very satisfied with this discovery, telling me that many non-native trees I'd see on the island were the result of a shipwreck, when the cargoes of non-native species, destined for elsewhere, washed ashore and ended up in our yards. Again I wondered: Whose house had been here, when did they leave, and where did they go?

On the walk back home, out of breath, Jack plunked his large frame down in the middle of a patch of poison ivy, which thrives on the island. "Watch out!" I tried to say before he sat. But Jack said he was not allergic, wasn't he lucky, and he laughed at me, who remained on my feet.

Five lights—a row of small panes of glass—were above south and north doors of original Bound Brook Island houses, i.e., those built between 1730 and mid-1800s. WHSM

"I think Bunting was the name of the family that lived in that house near the school," he said. "The house was flaked*—cut apart, the pieces numbered—and moved to town, either floated down the Herring River to its outlet in Wellfleet Harbor or carted to town by oxen and then rolled on timbers.

"Today you see Bound Brook houses mostly on the west end of Wellfleet. Usually you can tell it's a Bound Brook house by the five 'lights' above the front and back doors, those small panes of glass that let in light. Your house has them, mine too. And the Baker house down the road."

This small detail—the five lights—changed my experience of being in the town of Wellfleet: Whenever I saw a house with five lights over the front door—and there are many—I would know that house had begun its life on

---

* A glossary on page 145 explains this and many other likely-unfamiliar terms.

Bound Brook Island. I imagine that island carpenters Stephen and his son Joel Atwood decided to follow the style of the original Atwood house built in 1730 with its five lights.

So, at the Bunting's cellar hole I saw the evidence of the island's depopulation, and I soon learned that the community had suffered two irreversible losses. The islanders had relied on Duck Harbor's deep anchorage to the southwest to give them immediate access to the bay—to begin fishing voyages, which were their livelihood, and for transportation, which was easier and often faster by water than by land with its sandy or rutted roads. But by the mid-nineteenth century, Duck Harbor had silted up, and no boat could make it out to the bay. The second loss was that the land, already poor and eroded from more than a century of timber extraction and overgrazing by livestock, could no longer produce enough food to sustain the community. Family after family moved off the island, most flaking their houses and reassembling them in town.

THE BUNTING FAMILY LEAVES

Leaving the island! Leaving home!
Life had turned too hard, harbor
silted up, soil too poor to plant.
Pack up, like the others,
move it all to the village,
its large harbor, church, more neighbors.

Sarah called to the men flaking her house:
Careful with the windows! Careful with the lights!
As she walked beside the wagon,
holding Angeline's hand, she took
one last look:
the golden hill,
mulberry tree, lilac
and the hearthstone—
too heavy,
left behind.

Lombard Cemetery and Old Photographs

Another day Jack took me to an overlook I've always called "The Point." It's the farthest upland in northwest Bound Brook Island, overlooking South Truro. I learned later that this spit of land is actually beyond the Wellfleet border and is officially part of the neighboring town of Truro. Looking westward, the view of Cape Cod Bay as far as Provincetown is a breathtaking panorama. Below us, little Bound Brook, which gave the island its name, winds westward toward the bay but does not reach it. On a clear day it is a flat ribbon of blue, reflecting sky, surrounded by a vast, verdant marsh.

On the narrowest of footpaths, only six inches wide, we leave the view, threading through heather, bayberry, and blueberry, a veritable heath. After a while, once we are in the woods again, Jack takes a trail off to the right that leads to the tiny Lombard Cemetery. It's sited on the side of a wooded hill. Jack says the story is that Thomas Lombard and his children wanted to look southward from their South Truro house and see where wife and mother Mary Lombard, dead of smallpox at 44, was buried in 1859. The Truro townsmen had not allowed her body to be buried in the town cemetery due to fear of contagion. In 1859 the graveyard was visible from the Lombards' house, as all the land was bare of trees.

The Lombard Cemetery atop a hill in northwestern Bound Brook Island. Mary Lombard's stone is in sun; that of her husband and son appears in the shade at the right. 2019

Only two graves accompany Mary Lombard's: her son Thomas Jr., who died of consumption in 1870 at age 24, and husband Thomas, who died in 1873 at age 60. Both men's names and dates are carved into their one stone. I learned years later that another son, James, also died in 1870—"drowned at sea" said the Truro death records. Below his name, with the same date and cause of death, two more names: Atkins Rich, age 42, and Atkins Rich Jr., age 11. Time and again this happened as I delved into island life: I found stories, often sad ones, embedded in handwritten records, like this one, of three mariners dying together, drowned at sea. James's body was lost and could not be interred in the Lombard Cemetery.

"I hope the Park keeps up its promise to maintain this place," Jack says. All of Bound Brook Island is included in what became the Cape Cod National Seashore Park in 1961. He lifts a section of rusted pipe fencing and tries to restore it to a granite post, one of four enclosing this lonesome, weedy cemetery in the woods.

Another day Jack told me about how much the landscape had changed in the time he had lived on Bound Brook Island. In 1936, when he arrived here as a young man of 23, the hills were bare, not densely wooded as they are today. Back then you would be able to see the bay from the hill behind my house—not so today, with the line of sight blocked by stands of pitch pine and scrub oak.

This 1924 photo shows Jack's house at the far right, mine at the far lower left, Captain Baker's house in the distant middle, and the bay on the middle left, before revegetation occurred in the last century. WHSM

The first photograph of "old" Bound Brook that I ever saw was a print from 1903 that Jack had found in the "trash or treasures" shack at the Wellfleet transfer station. He gave me a copy, which I include below. Looking at it I had an eerie feeling of familiarity: two houses, the one on the lower left was mine, the other was Jack's across the way. The photograph was taken from the hill behind what is now my house. What was so shocking were the bare hills, an expanse of shaven contours and no roadside vegetation—totally opposite my experience of the island, where today's trees obscure all vistas.

After several years my hikes with Jack ended as age and increasing imbalance stopped him from bushwhacking the woods. He kept at his painting in his studio. He was known for oil portraits of his ancestors as he imagined them, but my favorite painting was a haunting abstract he called *The Big Blow*.

Two houses in a bare Bound Brook Island landscape; the photographer faces north. 1903

THE BIG BLOW
for Jack

The falls are sudden. In a flash
your six-four frame's down. Flat.

Memory always served: all those stories.
Now memory is lace the weather filters through.

You work this last painting, all grays and black.
You obsess in the cluttered splattered space.

"The Big Blow" you call it. A Wellfleet
storm raging, destructive, obliterating?

An argument gone catastrophic?
A fight to the utter black and blue?

A long life falling apart, summoning
in paint its full force to protest.

Jack kept a daybook in which he recorded his doings, each day, on a single page. He also sometimes wrote down his memories of Bound Brook Island: stories about the last "Native woman," as he called her, the whalebone fencepost at the Atwood-Higgins property, the sign that said "Delight" salvaged from a Provincetown tourist house and that he mounted above the kitchen door on the Baker property he owned for more than a decade. We'd sit at the table in front of his large north window, and we would talk. How I wish I could sit there with him again.

John "Jack" Hughes Hall, 1913–2003
Photo courtesy of Katrina Hall

2

———

How This Island of Hills
and Ravines Formed

AS I WRITE, I feel tension between two impulses. The first is my desire to render the mythic quality of place—Bound Brook Island's beauty, quietude, physical uniqueness, history of abandonment, and mystery. The second is my obsessive, pleasure-filled search to answer my cascade of questions about the island's geology, ecology, history, and inhabitants. My hope is that I will bring you along with me as I pursue and explore what fascinates me.

Topography

What first captivated me about Bound Brook Island? The land itself. Ins and outs, steep ups and downs, as if crenellated land had been pressed together. As I walked on trails with Jack Hall, I felt the landscape in my bones and muscles and drank it in with my eyes. Rendered on a Google map, the terrain looks pocked like the surface of the moon.

Bound Brook Island's hummocky, up-and-down topography is glacial in origin. Its *kames*, knolls or hills, were created when gravel and sand (glacial

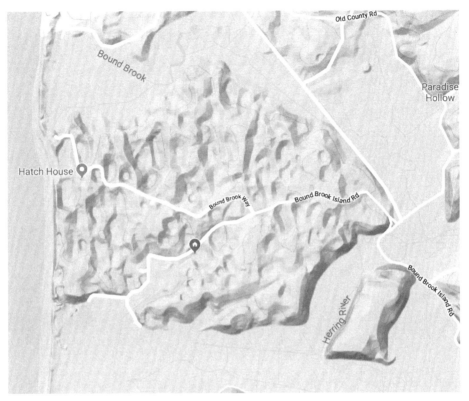

Terrain of Bound Book Island. Google Maps

drift) were embedded in ice and left in mounds when the glacial ice melted. And it has *kettles*, depressions, sites where gigantic ice blocks were buried by glacial drift, sometimes for thousands of years. The weight of the ice pressed into the land. If the land was pushed lower than the water table, the kettle sapped water and became a pond—this is the origin of the many swimmable kettle ponds of Wellfleet. Almost all the small kettles on Bound Brook Island are now dry.

What forces created this striking topography of hills, dales, and ravines? Knobby terrain is not everywhere on the Cape—it's here on Bound Brook, somewhat on Griffin's Island immediately south, north in some of Truro, and in a few other locations. Specific geological forces concentrated on the land that is now Bound Brook Island.

The Geology of Bound Brook Island

Compared with the vastness of Earth's age in geologic time, all of Cape Cod is very young. It was created only about 19,000 years ago, as the last ice age's glacier, the Laurentide Ice Sheet, melted, "retreated" northward, and scraped Cape Cod into being. (By comparison, the land that is now Boston was pressed into the New England landmass 380 million years ago.)

The Laurentide Ice Sheet began its descent from Canada 25,000 years ago as the Earth warmed. It achieved its farthest advance, shown on the map below, left, around 23,000 years ago. At that time, the northeast coastal plain of land extended almost 100 miles beyond most of what is now the coast of New England, shown below, right. This immense plain, later known as the Continental Shelf, was well vegetated and provided a home to animals including mastodons, mammoths, deer, and moose, among others. So much water was locked up in the northern ice cap and glaciers that the sea level dropped to at least 300 feet lower than it is today, exposing much more landmass, for millennia.

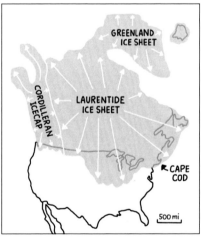

Maximum extent of the Laurentide Ice Sheet

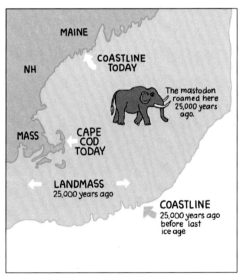

Extent of the Continental Shelf 25,000 years ago, the vast plain of earth supporting vegetation and wildlife

As it descended from the north, the Laurentide Ice Sheet was a half-mile thick over the area that is now Cape Cod. Three massive lobes of ice were directly involved in shaping Cape Cod and the islands of Nantucket and Martha's Vineyard.

Continued warming ended this last ice age. The glacial ice lobes began to melt and retreat northward; the sea level rose. This happened fairly quickly—by 18,000 years ago, the lobes had disappeared from the area shown below.

The juncture of two retreating melting lobes, the South Channel Lobe and the Cape Cod Bay Lobe, created enormous stress to the land below, what is now the forearm of our Cape Cod. Tremendous forces— the northward scraping movement caused by retreating ice, the enormous weight of the lobes, and the flowing melted water—formed the Outer Cape, which includes Bound Brook Island.

The land that is now Bound Brook was close to the very seam where the two giant lobes of ice were retreating north, melting, pressing, scraping. This small bit of land was also flooded for hundreds of years by the meltwater of the South Channel Lobe.

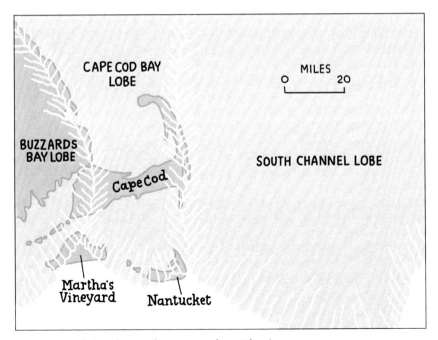

Three lobes of glacial ice at the Laurentide Ice Sheet's farthest reach. After Oldale and Barlow, 1986

It seems likely that the melting waters carved out the long, slender hollows of Wellfleet and Truro, although there are other theories about their creation. All these hollows slant on an east–west parallel on our maps: the Herring River valley, the Pamet valley of Truro, Lombard Hollow, Prince Valley, and Paradise Hollow. The meltwater coursed over the entirety of Bound Brook Island, gouging the deep ravines that exist there today. This meltwater created huge deltas flowing toward what is now saltwater Cape Cod Bay but at that time was becoming Glacial Lake Cape Cod, made up entirely of fresh water melted from the glacier.

For a long while the existence of a Glacial Lake Cape Cod was a hypothesis. However, in a pit dug in the twentieth century at the eastern side of Bound Brook Island, near the road onto the island, US Geodetic Survey geologist Robert Oldale and his team found "large-scale deltaic foreset bedding." This was evidence, Oldale told me, of a huge stream of water. The meltwater of the lobes, flooding east to west, deposited great amounts of sediment. Immense amounts of fresh water streamed westward over Bound Brook Island, as it did over other land on the Outer Cape, helping to create Glacial Lake Cape Cod.

What happened to this huge freshwater lake? It's assumed that, as melting continued, the lake finally overflowed and drained "catastrophically" through

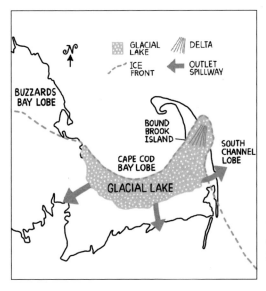

Glacial Lake Cape Cod.
Adapted from Larson and
Stone, 1982

the Cape's lowest points—where the Cape Cod Canal is now, and perhaps south of Barnstable as well as out through Orleans. (See the arrows on the map opposite.) With the full retreat of the glacier and the higher sea level caused by glacial melt, Atlantic Ocean waters filled the space that was Glacial Lake Cape Cod, and that space became Cape Cod Bay.

Finally, I had my answer. Bound Brook's topography was unusual because powerful geologic forces had worked upon this small piece of land. Two gigantic ice lobes had pressed it, moved over it, and then overwhelmed it with meltwater rushing to "create" Glacial Lake Cape Cod. Like elsewhere in Wellfleet, large chunks of glacier left behind sat on the land and created kettles, smooth bowls in the terrain, like the one right outside my house. No wonder the terrain map looked more pocked than the moon that I saw through my binoculars. No wonder every hike challenged me with steep climbs and descents.

The finishing touch: After the very last of the ice retreated, at least a thousand years of winds whipped and deposited aeolian layers on top of the glacial drift. This is why, all over Bound Brook Island, if you scrape aside the detritus of pine needles and leaves, you find sand, beige and fine-grained.

BIRTH OF BOUND BROOK ISLAND

Ice, water, rock, wind, sand
birthed this small "island."
The hills are rubble—gravel,
boulders, stone—left
by the behemoth glacier
as it scraped, weeping, north.

Have a look at this stone
I teased from an exposed
bank of sand—a *ventifact*
—its irregular facets
abraded and smoothed
by the fierce winds
of the Pleistocene.

Every place on Earth has its geologic story—how it came to be where it is and how it was formed. What I learned about Bound Brook Island confirmed my intuition: Its formation was dramatic—perhaps unique on Cape Cod—at the juncture of two glacial lobes, later aswirl in pounding waters as a glacial lake formed. Its hillocks and steep valleys, its dusting of aeolian sand, tell a tale I hear every time I go walking.

3

Nausets, Pamets, Punonakanits, and Colonists

EIGHTEEN MEN CLIMBED DOWN from the *Mayflower* and boarded its shallop—a small, open, wooden shallow-draft boat—on a cold December day in 1620. They sailed south from the Provincetown harbor along the Cape Cod Bay shore. It had taken the *Mayflower*'s carpenter over two weeks to reassemble the shallop's pieces, which passengers had used for beds as they crossed the Atlantic Ocean. In earlier forays on foot the "discoverers" had found a freshwater spring, a pond, a river, a hill where corn was stored in baskets "very handsomely and cunningly made," as well as a European kettle, abandoned huts, and graves. These men had found the belongings of the Pamet people, part of the Nauset tribe, who inhabited the area now known as Truro.

On their many-day trip in the shallop starting on December 6 the men reported "the water froze on our clothes and made them . . . like coats of iron." The party of "discovery" sailed past Bound Brook Island. At that time the island was inhabited by other members of the Nauset tribe, who were called Punonakanits after the area where they settled, now Wellfleet. Most of the Nausets moved inland, away from the shore, for the winter, so it's unlikely a Punonakanit scout would have sighted the shallop from the island's dunes.

The "discoverers" did encounter Nauset men farther south on the shore cutting up a pilot whale and later skirmished with others on what is now called First Encounter Beach.

The Englishmen in the shallop beheld a landscape heavily forested with oak and white pine, with smaller areas of birch, beech, red maple, hickory, and cherry. "Wooded to the brink of the sea" is the description of the Cape in *Mourt's Relation,* published in London in 1622. The shallop sailed in a curve around the bay and eventually arrived at an abandoned place called Patuxet by the people who once lived there; the "discoverers" explored the harbor and its many streams that supplied drinking water. On December 12, they sailed straight across Cape Cod Bay, back to the *Mayflower,* with the news of this good place to settle, which they named Plymouth.

The Punonakanits

In 2012, archaeologists working under the auspices of the Cape Cod National Seashore took samples from a grid of hundreds of bores into the Bound Brook Island property where Captain David Baker Jr. built his house in the late 1700s. At the site of the most promising exploratory bore they found a remarkable trove: arrowheads, tools of stone, and a shellfish midden—evidence of thousands of years of habitation of the Punonakanits. The archaeologists also found coins and shards of pottery left by the Baker family (dating from the late 1700s through 1882). In his boyhood, Stephen Biddle, of the last family that privately owned the property, collected countless arrowheads when he visited his grandparents, Francis and Katherine Biddle, who bought the Baker house in 1949 from Jack Hall.

Thinking about these finds, I came to see how well situated this particular site, once the Punonakanits' and then the Baker family's, was for habitation—close to the bay, yet entirely sheltered from storms by a large hill on the west and north. The bay waters, which might have flowed closer to the Baker house than they do today, provided prodigious amounts of shellfish and finned fish, as well as beached pilot whales, for consumption as food and other uses. A freshwater spring located a three-minute walk north supplied drinking water.

I am sure an archaeologist could dig on my property (I know just the spot) and find evidence of long-ago inhabitants. When we walk on what looks like ordinary earth, we touch the past of so many other souls underfoot.

Some say the first people came to Cape Cod as much as 9,000 years ago, following the wild animals they hunted. By 5,000 years ago, they had arrived at their pattern of agricultural settlement, remaining for about 12 years in one place until relocating for fresh soils and hunting grounds. A lethal disease, now thought to be leptospirosis (transmitted by bacteria from rat urine), brought by European traders and fishermen in 1614–1617, devastated Cape Cod's indigenous peoples. (Ninety percent of the Patuxet people of what became Plymouth died, leaving that area abandoned, ready for the English to claim.) The Punonakanits, their social fabric torn by disease and the newcomers' privatization of land, had likely abandoned Bound Brook by the mid-1700s. Captain Baker chose to build his house around 1800 on land that had been cleared, cultivated, and lived upon by Punonakanit people.

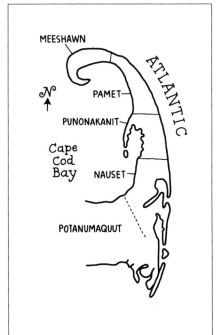

Areas native peoples were inhabiting in 1620 on the Outer Cape; these groups were all part of the Wampanoag Federation of southern Massachusetts and Rhode Island.

How the Island Got Its Name

This tract extended from the northern limits of Nauset to a little brook called by the Indians Sapokonisk and by the English Bound Brook. . . . —Plymouth Colony Records, 1666

Gazing from the overlook named "The Point," in the northwest I could see a blue stream curving among the reeds, reflecting sky, eddying short of the grass-topped dunes that line Cape Cod Bay. That's how the brook got its name, I assumed: Because those dunes *lock* the brook from the bay, the brook is *bound* by the dunes.

But, no: On the oldest maps I gathered, no dune blocked the stream. Instead, the brook flowed to the bay. It was a tidal inlet flushed by saltwater twice a day. Eventually, I read in a local history that in the early eighteenth century, mariners rowed their boats from the bay up the waters of little Bound Brook with the tide. Indeed, the fact that Bound Brook was an outlet to the sea explains why several sea captains, including Thomas Hopkins Sr., Reuben Rich, and Richard Atwood, settled in the northwestern and northern parts of the island in the late 1700s and early 1800s.

In the 1640s, a group of men from the original Plymouth Colony, finding that Plymouth soil had become too depleted for farming, crossed the bay to acquire more fertile land. Henry David Thoreau relates the story in his 1865 book *Cape Cod*. After purchasing land in Nauset (now Eastham and Orleans) from the Nauset people, the English inquired about the land more northerly, in what is now Wellfleet. "Whose land is this?" they asked. George, the sachem—political leader—replied, "No one's." The English said, "Then it is ours," and George agreed. The English held the lands for years without paying for them.

However, in 1666 the leader of the Punonakanits, Lieutenant Anthony, who had assumed an English name and honorific, claimed Punonakanit, the territory that is now Wellfleet. The English then purchased a large amount of land from Lieutenant Anthony, who, however, reserved for himself a neck of land today called Indian Neck; another neck called Lieutenant Island was named for him but settled by the English. The northern-most boundary of the newly purchased colonial lands was a brook whose native name was Sapokonisk, meaning "miry field" or "wet outlet." The little brook was the northern boundary of certain English holdings, so they named it Bound Brook. Today, the brook is still the rough bound—*boundary*—between Truro and Wellfleet. So that is the origin of the name—having to do with boundary, *not* with being bound away from the bay (which did happen, but many decades after the name Bound Brook was bestowed).

In 1712 the Truro town record relates that selectmen set out to renew the boundary: "We went to look for the ancient mentioned Bound at the Mouth of Boundbrook [*sic*]; but the white oak tree with Stones about it we could not find; and judge it may be washed away by the Sea." Thus, early on, the obliterating nature of the sea was obvious. Surveyors set "a new Stone in the Ground, with several Stones laid about it—on top of the Hill due East from the place where we judge the former Bound stood." Perhaps this pile of stones is still there, overgrown by heather.

Land Acquisition, a Defiled Landscape

The English farmers who relocated from Plymouth to Nauset in the early 1640s cleared forest there and planted corn. Their plows dug deeper and turned over more soil than the Nauset people's tools and thus depleted the soil more quickly, exposing it to the air. That is why in the later 1600s, having exhausted the Nauset soils just as they had exhausted Plymouth soils, farmers looked north on the bayside to the area now known as Wellfleet, including Bound Brook Island, for arable land and pasturage.

On Bound Brook, both the uplands suitable for settlement and livestock grazing and the low-lying meadows rich with salt hay used as winter fodder were granted to several individuals of high status and to newcomers called "allowed inhabitants." Parcels were sold and bought in a lively market of real estate transactions. However, until 1730 or so, the land was used for pasturage and for investment, not yet for settling families.

Meanwhile, settlers everywhere on the Cape harvested the old forests to the point of depletion: the King's Navy requisitioned prime timber (trees at least 4 feet in diameter and 100 feet high) for ship masts; settlers built houses, barns, and fences, and they cut wood for fuel. By the 1780s, St. John de Crevecoeur wrote: "I am at a loss to conceive what the inhabitants live on besides clams, oysters and fish; their piney lands being the most ungrateful soil in the world." By 1794 a visitor commented, "The land is barren." The few stands of wood that remained were pitch pine and scrub oak.

What else had happened to the land, in addition to overtilling and deforestation? Overgrazing. In 1768 the Province of the Massachusetts Bay passed a law that no one was to drive their horses, cattle, or sheep to feed upon the shores and beaches of Bound Brook Island and Griffin's Island between April 1 and the end of November. Livestock was consuming all the vegetation that kept the sandy soil in place:

> The ground is much broken and damnified [sic], and the sands
> blown on said islands and meadows adjoining, to the great dam-
> age, not only of the proprietors of the said islands in their prop-
> erty, but also to the said district in general, as it will greatly
> endanger a great valuable tract of salt marsh belonging to the in-
> habitants of said district; as also, in the process of time, fill up the
> Herring River, and destroy the navigation thereof.

These last words about destroying navigation were prophetic, as we shall see later. Immediately, though, fines were set for each kind of animal trespass (cattle, five shillings a head; horses and sheep, one shilling a head—in 2021 dollars, $45 and $9 respectively), and property owners erected pens to hold their animals. However, that legislation pertained only to the beaches and shores of Bound Brook Island. What of the rest of the island?

Wellfleet's town records give us an idea of how much livestock was grazing in Wellfleet. Between 1767 and 1794, thirty men each registered a unique earmark for identifying their large holdings of sheep, cattle, and swine. The names of many of these men we see still see in Wellfleet today as street names: Atwood, Baker, Holbrook, Hopkins, Arey, and Gross. Here is one entry:

> Thomas Holbrook's Mark for Neat Cattle, Sheep & Swine is a Crop
> of the Right Ear and a Slitt [sic] in the End of the Left Ear. Wellfleet
> 19th Sept 1768   Recorded by John Greenough, Dist. Clerk

From Wellfleet Town Records

Over the years these flocks and herds ate most of the vegetation from the hills and dales of Bound Brook and elsewhere in Wellfleet, leading to erosion of topsoil and to decades when nothing would grow. The flocks and the herds soon were no more. By the mid-1800s, a typical Bound Brook household had only one horse, maybe one pig, one to three cattle, and no sheep, because there was no vegetation left for them to graze. In 1850, only Henry Atwood owned a pair of oxen. The bare landscape is still evident in photos from the early twentieth century (see pages 15 and 16).

In the span of a century and a half, from 1640 to 1790, Bound Brook Island went from heavily forested to denuded. This condition lasted until the mid-twentieth century, when slowly a new cover of growth rose, so that today Bound Brook Island is quite green—not with the large variety of hardwoods of its past, but with pitch pines, oaks, bearberry, the rugosa rose, and thick bushes.

Today, amber carpets of "wavy hair grass" *(Deschampsia flexuosa)* grow below the branches of pitch pines and oaks. Their stalks stand about a foot high, with tiny seed heads, like midges, that dance in the breezes and glimmer in sunlight. This hardy yet delicate grass grows in the shallow, sandy soil of Bound Brook Island, soil that most other grasses would not tolerate. Bound Brook Island, like much of Cape Cod, is an example of the degradation of land by practices that consumed resources for present-day needs with no vision of the future.

Shore Whaling

Today, rarely does a whale leave the Atlantic Ocean for Cape Cod Bay—perhaps a stray wanders in, lost or wounded. The leviathan will beach and die, its huge, decaying carcass to be dealt with by the National Park Service and local authorities.

But in the 1600s and 1700s, pods of many hundreds of small pilot whales from the Atlantic routinely swam around the tip of the Cape into the bay, hungrily pursuing squid and bottom-feeding fish such as cod. An entirely different idea of the bay comes to mind: waters filled with much more sea life than we experience today. How I would like to witness, when I look up from reading my book on Bound Brook beach, a pod of pilot whales cavorting.

The Nausets, including the Punonakanits, harvested these pilot whales, called "blackfish" by the English colonists. A blackfish was about 15 feet long and weighed four to five tons. The Nausets not only made use of the oil but also ate the meat, which was the color of beef, and they harvested all parts of the whale's anatomy for tools and materials. The colonists sought whale oil to fuel their lamps.

Sometimes, hundreds of blackfish inexplicably stranded themselves on the shore, and Bound Brook men slaughtered them as they had been taught to by the Nausets. They boiled the blubber in try pots, huge metal cauldrons set up over fires on the beach. Men and boys did the trying, the women bringing food and other supplies. Soon, the need and market for whale oil required the colonists to take more active measures rather than wait for the random beaching of a blackfish pod.

On the earliest maps of Bound Brook Island, a whale lookout tower stands in the west near the Baker house, on a high point overlooking the Cape Cod Bay waters. The alarm was called out when pods of blackfish were spotted swimming far off. Men rowed out in skiffs to drive the creatures to the beach; thus, "shore whaling" as an industry got under way on the island.

The trying of pilot whale blubber in pots on New England beaches took place mostly before the age of the camera. I was able to find one engraved image, from a magazine in 1885, that shows men at their try pots on a beach on Long Island, New York.

One artifact of shore whaling days remains today on Bound Brook. It's a try shack, a small wooden building that once sat at the back of the beach and stored all the trying equipment used to harvest oil. Enormous quantities of smoke wafted over and around it as blubber was tried, time and time again, for decades. With the thinning of the blackfish stock and no further demand for whale oil, the shore whaling industry ended. I believe that the Baker family

Trying whale oil on a beach on Long Island, New York; image from the cover of Harper's Young People *magazine, February 1885*

moved the try shack up from the beach and set it next to their house. Frugal Cape Codders, having no local availability of timber, often repurposed existing wooden structures. When the Biddle family occupied the one-time Baker house, the little try house became their guest quarters.

Jack Hall told me that this neat building (see photo on page 119) is the oldest structure on the island; its timbers date back to the 1600s. Interestingly, there is no federal financial support for researching the age of a structure that has been relocated, as this little try shack was. Assessing the age of the Bakers's house was government supported because the house was built on the site where it currently stands.

BLACKFISH

I have seen nearly four hundred at one time lying dead on the shore. —The Reverend Levi Whitman, 1794

When the lookout on Bound Brook's hill cried *Blackfish! Ahoy!*
men with blowing horns, lances, harpoons, rowed out to corral
blackfish bucking like horses and drive them wounded to shore.

Not fish but pilot whales, four to five tons each full grown,
fifteen feet long, *shining black, like India-rubber* said Thoreau
who walked by the dead in the bloody water.

Men stripped blubber, dragged it
to try pots to render oil—one whale, one gallon—
prized as soot-less fuel for lamps, oil for delicate clocks.

Headless carcasses rotted, turned to stink
on the beach till the tides swept them away.
The blackfish dwindled, fewer each year.

When black oil spewed inland, shore whaling ended.
Here, though, a relic of blackfish days: this try house, the island's
oldest structure, moved from beach, up this hill.

No try pots stored here, no fishing gear leaning against the walls.
The velvety black on this board? Touch here—this trace
of oily smoke. You've touched the death of whales.

Today, a restaurant in Truro is named Blackfish. I can shop in an upscale stationer's store and purchase greeting cards picturing blackfish and other whales. But I have never seen a blackfish in Cape Cod Bay, and I don't expect I ever will.

And what of the Punonakanits, the Nausets? All that seems to remain in Wellfleet of those who flourished here for millennia, with the mammals and fishes of the sea and surrounded by old forests, are a few place and street names, including Pamet, Chequessett, Anawam, Nauhaught, and Massasoit. Fortunately, it's a different story for the Wampanoag Nation; five bands live in Massachusetts today, on Martha's Vineyard and the mainland, and 1993 saw the founding of the Wampanoag Language Reclamation Project.

Black Fish driven ashore at South Wellfleet, Cape Cod, Mass. About 1500 in the school. Sold for fifteen thousand dollars, which was divided among 300 inhabitants.

A Wellfleet postcard shows pilot whales on shore in a mass beaching in the early twentieth century.

4

Early Settlers, 1730 Onward

UPSTAIRS, IN A CHILD-SIZE BEDROOM of our Bound Brook Island house, the previous owner had tacked to a wall the 1958 US Geodetic Survey topographical map of Wellfleet. I peered at the map, which was faded after so many years, learning the shape of the island, its roads, footpaths, wetlands, and the location of the nine houses that existed there in 1958.

Soon enough, I visited the Wellfleet Historical Society, where I found many older maps, mostly from the nineteenth century, framed on its walls. As I turned a tight corner on my way to the second floor, I encountered a large, framed pastel rendering of Bound Brook Island by artist Joan Hopkins Coughlin. The mostly vivid-green pastel was based on a memory map by her great-uncle Dr. Nehemiah Somes Hopkins, born in 1860, who had lived on Bound Brook as a boy. Years later I came across Dr. Hopkins's original memory map, rendered in his own hand. Not nine, but twenty little white houses dotted the landscape, with the householder's name written under each little house. My house and Jack Hall's were labeled "E. Atwood" and "H. Atwood," respectively, and the map displayed features such as swamps, a windmill, saltworks, harbor, a salt lick, and a schoolhouse. What happened to this community? I wondered. Where had these houses gone?

I know today's Bound Brook Island—where no one lives year-round. But Dr. Hopkins's memory map showed me a populated Bound Brook Island—a community of mariner and farmer families, one of the earliest settlements in Wellfleet. Eventually I would scour handwritten town and county records, US Censuses, and early maps to learn more about the people who lived on the island over a span of seven generations.

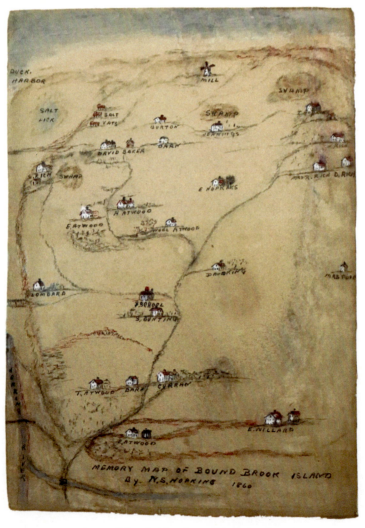

Memory Map of Bound Brook Island in 1860, drawn by Nehemiah Somes Hopkins in 1939. WHSM, gift of Al Kraft

For about 100 years, Bound Brook Island was used as pasturage by English settlers who lived in Nauset. The first family didn't settle on the island until around 1730. I offer vignettes of three of its early settlers: Thomas Higgins, Captain Reuben Rich, and Captain David Baker—briefly telling their story and their family's story through time. I regret that I can provide no vignettes of women. Women were not even listed by name for the first 50 years of the US Census. We can imagine their labor at the homestead, in childbearing and childrearing, in food preparation and storage, gardening, laundering, weaving, and sewing. Their primary record is in the handwritten town ledgers: birth, marriage, the births and deaths of their children, and their own death.

Thomas Higgins Builds a House

Shortly after you arrive on Bound Brook Island, you pass a modest twentieth-century shingled house on your left. In the past, a National Park Service ranger lived there with his family. Continue a few hundred yards until just before the tarred road turns to sand, and park your vehicle. Walk down the long drive-way on the left, past a few weather-worn, rustic, twentieth-century structures, until you see a yellow-beige Cape house below you: That's the Atwood-Higgins House. The Cape Cod National Seashore—the National Park Service—now manages the 24-acre Atwood-Higgins Historical District.

The Atwood-Higgins House, showing traditional clapboard on its south face. 2020

Higgins family lore puts the construction date of the house at 1635 or so, but that date has not been borne out by archaeological study of the house materials. Instead, it's believed that around 1730, Thomas Higgins, then in his late twenties, built a small "half Cape" (having a door and two windows on one side—the right side of the house shown on page 37) on a small plateau situated above the Herring River. He was the great-grandson of Richard Higgins, one of the seven colonists who had left the Plymouth Colony for Nauset across the bay to pioneer and stake out new fertile farmland.

Thomas Higgins, his wife Abigail, and eventually their eight children were likely the first permanent English settlers on Bound Brook. I am sure Thomas Higgins chose this well-endowed spot on the plateau because Punonakanits had cleared it and had lived here. The Herring River below, wide and deep enough for shipbuilding, supplied fish and fresh water in abundance, and the lands above the house could be farmed.

Solomon Higgins, born in 1743, inherited the house; he was a sea captain and a veteran of the Revolutionary War. As was customary at the time, several generations lived under one roof. They included Solomon and his wife, two of their unmarried children, the five members of his son Solomon Jr.'s family, and Solomon's older brother and his wife, who were in their seventies. That's eleven souls in a half Cape house—about 500 square feet of living space. Perhaps this arrangement was workable only because the men and boys often were away on sea voyages. Around 1800, plans were made to build onto the house, creating the "full Cape house" we see today, with its two windows on each side of the south- and north-facing doors.

Three more people were housed somewhere on the Higgins property—Blacks, as noted in the 1800 census. The entry was posted in the column titled "All Other Free Persons"—not in the final column, "Slaves." Whether the three constituted a small family or three farmhands is unknown. Two other Wellfleet households in that census also listed Blacks as free, and there are no listings for enslaved people. In that year Wellfleet's population was 1,207, of whom nine were Black.

In 1805 the Higgins family sold the house to Captain Thomas Atwood. Because of successive ownership, there is more to the Atwood-Higgins connection than the hyphen that links the names. Thomas Atwood's mother was a Higgins. Thomas Atwood and Solomon Higgins both were direct descendents of Richard Higgins, the pioneer. Buyer and seller were distant cousins.

Historian Shebnah Rich tells a tale about Thomas Atwood from the days when most Bound Brook Island mariners were whaling captains. It was 1810, and a boat from South Truro had "fastened" to a right whale that thrashed in a huge circuit and could not be brought in. A messenger was dispatched for retired Captain Tom Atwood, who was at home reading his Bible. Atwood grabbed his equipment and, Rich writes, "He was soon in the boat . . . gave his orders according to her maneuvers, was rowed to the *safe side* and sent his lance to her life."

In 1825 Captain Tom sold the house to his son Thomas Jr. I have a photocopy of six pages handwritten by the grandson of David Curran, who lived in a house close to the Atwoods' home after 1850. Curran wrote, "No church was ever built on the Island, and all who wanted to worship traveled to the town of Wellfleet or Truro. Thomas and Mercy Atwood went to church in a two-wheeled one-horse chaise. At full tide the thatch often floated under the horse's belly as they crossed the meadow from Bound Brook Island to Merrick's Island. The journey and services took the entire day. They either carried their lunch or were guests of someone in the village."

Thomas Atwood died in 1873; his widow, Mercy, died seven years later. The house was closed up and remained vacant for decades until George K. Higgins, a distant relative of the early owners, assumed ownership in 1919 and began developing the property as a summer residence.

Over the next quarter century Higgins built several rustic structures on his property. To achieve his building plans, he twice had the town of Wellfleet relocate Bound Brook Island Road to a more northerly route—the original cart road ran close to the main house.

———

You can still walk the original road. Look for a rail fence on the left almost immediately as you travel the road up onto Bound Brook Island. Walk past that fence and follow the footpath, which was once the old road. In short order you will arrive on the Atwood-Higgins property, with the Cape house itself sited off

to the left, down an incline. The now-dilapidated twentieth-
century structures George Higgins built will be on your right.

———

In 1961, George Higgins gave his extensive Bound Brook holdings, totaling more than 600 acres, to the newly established Cape Cod National Seashore. Today, weekly tours of the Atwood-Higgins house in summer by the National Park Service offer a window into life in another age.

Captain Reuben Rich Builds a Schooner

The first person who truly captured my interest in my years of reading about Bound Brook was Captain Reuben Rich, born in 1748, whose house was in the northwest of the island. His father, Deacon Reuben Rich, was a selectman in 1763 when the Northern District of Eastham, after petitioning for 30 years, separated from Eastham and finally established itself as an independent town named Wellfleet.

Captain Reuben Rich was a man of imagination and force. Well before 1800 he is said to have built Wellfleet's first wharf, on Griffin's Island (just south of Bound Brook Island) opposite White Hill, where the Herring River could be forded at low tide. Near the wharf, fish could be packed for shipment. At the wharf, vessels arriving from the West Indies unloaded cargoes of sugar, molasses, and other goods onto oxcarts for distribution. This enterprise was the early making of Rich's fortune. It should be noted that these cargoes were elements of the slave trade—salted fish from Cape Cod fed the enslaved Africans toiling in Caribbean fields; by return ship, West Indian harvests and products were transported north for sale.

In 1799, Rich financed and oversaw the construction of the first schooner in Wellfleet. His *Freemason* was built immediately below the Atwood-Higgins house on Bound Brook, on the Herring River, of black locust wood harvested from the steep hillside. The newly launched ship, capable of 100-ton burden, sailed down the then-robust Herring River at high tide into Wellfleet Bay.

Enoch Pratt's history relates that in 1802, of the 25 vessels owned by Wellfleet men, five were engaged in whale fishery at the straits of Belle Isle and

Newfoundland. Each vessel carried a crew of about 14 men. Of the five vessels, the largest was a 100-ton burden schooner—it was probably Captain Rich's *Freemason*. The ship carried its own preserving salt aboard. If the crew could not try enough whale blubber to fully load up with oil, they made up the voyage with a cargo of codfish, salted in barrels.

I wondered why Reuben Rich had named his schooner *Freemason*. To track down the answer, I visited Wellfleet's Adams Masonic Lodge, which was established in 1797. Concord's Paul Revere, Grand Master of Masons of Massachusetts, signed the Adams charter. The lodge, set high on a hill in the heart of Wellfleet, offers tours, and it sponsors weekly community dinners of lobster and corn-on-the-cob in the summer months, fundraising for its charitable work.

Wellfleet's Adams Masonic Lodge today, high on a hill at 2 Bank Street

A member of both the Adams Lodge in Wellfleet and the Hiram Lodge in Provincetown told me that the orders' membership records are confidential; I could therefore not verify that Reuben Rich was a Mason. In 1821 the Lodge in Wellfleet surrendered its charter—it had held no meetings since 1812 and was in arrears in dues. In 1865, however, the charter was restored, and the first Grand Master installed was Naphtali Rich Jr., Reuben Rich's grandson. This leads me to believe that my hunch that Reuben Rich was a committed, proud Mason is correct.

Reuben Rich and several neighbors in Bound Brook Island's northwest established a total of nine new roads, cart paths really, on the island in 1799 and 1800. They walked the land, putting out stones and stakes for markers, and presented exact, written plans to Wellfleet selectmen. The selectmen had to approve and authorize payment to the landowners who were ceding portions of their holdings for these public rights of way.

One new road ran to the extensive salt hay meadows, whose harvest sustained each family's livestock. The most vital new cart path, however, connected inhabitants in the island's northwest to Duck Harbor to the south. The slow closing up of the island's bay access via the northern stream called Bound Brook in the late 1700s and early 1800s might have prompted mariners living in the northwest to create a road to Duck Harbor in the south. Duck Harbor would be their new access to the bay, access that was vital for those with marine livelihoods and for travel.

The community on Bound Brook Island was always oriented to the sea. Water travel was the best means to reach the growing community near Duck Creek in Wellfleet or beyond because travel by horseback, wagon, or stagecoach took far longer. The great majority of Bound Brook's men were mariners, and the bounty of the sea, rather than the land, provided their living. Generally, mariners turned to farming after they retired from seafaring. In the eighteenth century, Bound Brook mariners departed for whaling voyages, but whaling stopped entirely during the years of the American Revolution because of the British Navy's blockade. Once the war was over, the whaling fleet, through disuse, was irreparable. Fishing for cod, and eventually mackerel, on smaller vessels became the main occupation of Bound Brook's seafarers. Access to Duck Harbor was essential to their maritime livelihoods.

Reuben Rich married once, at age 54, in 1802—marriage at this advanced age was not typical for his time. Perhaps he had been too busy with his entrepreneurial enterprises and his many sea voyages to wed earlier. He and his wife Anna Thayer had three daughters, the eldest of whom, Anna, married Naphtali Rich (not closely related) from neighboring Truro. It is Naphtali Rich's name we see on the many nineteenth-century Bound Brook maps and listings—and some folk credit him with being an original island settler. But no, he came by the house in northwest Bound Brook through his wife's inheritance.

Near the end of his life, Captain Reuben Rich participated in the War of 1812 as a sanctioned privateer. With two other men he outfitted a vessel; the crew captured a British merchant ship on their first day out and brought the prize to Boston. He secured $17,000 ($265,000 in year 2021 dollars) for the sale of his interest. He died a few years later in 1819, at age 71. Two Bound Brook families named sons to honor him.

Reuben Rich's will extended to many handwritten pages, as he owned much property. To his wife Anna he gave many parcels of cleared land and salt meadow, fruit from the orchard, and water from the well, but only the eastern half of his dwelling house. That included half of the kitchen and one-third of the cellar, "with the right to go orderly in and out, and a right in the Porch to do her washing and spinning with the heirs"—his daughters. To his sister he gave five dollars a year for 10 years. "I give to my Brother Elisha a suit of Clothes such as he shall make a choice of out of all my wearing apparel to consist of one Hat, one handkerchief, one Surtout or Great coat, two shirts, one body coat, one waist coat, one pair breeches or small clothes, two pair of stockings. . . . I give to my nephew Reuben Rich all my Sea instruments and Sea books. . . . I give to my daughter Anna Rich my great Bible."

After Reuben's death and his wife's, daughter Anna and her family occupied the house, followed by her widower, Naphtali Rich, who died in 1887. Records from 1900 show the Rich house was purchased, disassembled, and moved north to Truro by Burton S. Hart, though I've been unable to find it or determine its fate. Hart eventually married into the Whitman family and developed what became years later the Whitman House restaurant on Great Hollow Road in Truro.

Captain Reuben Rich was buried in Wellfleet's Duck Creek Cemetery, but his daughter Anna and her husband were buried in South Truro, as were five of their eight children who did not survive beyond the age of two.* Why was Anna's family laid to rest in South Truro? The Rich family lived on the northern boundary with Truro, and Anna's husband had been born in Truro. From the Rich house it was easier to walk or ride to Truro than it was to journey south to the town of Wellfleet, so for Bound Brookers living in the north of the island, social and religious ties with Truro folk were strong.

Captain David Baker: The Duck Harbor & Beach Company—and the Family Saltworks

The large antique house that now nestles unseen as you drive the largest curve of Bound Brook Island Road was built around 1795. Full-grown trees along the road hide it from view, but before these established themselves you would have been able to see the house from mine. I imagine the Baker family chose this site because—once again—the Punonakanit people had lived in this prime spot that is sheltered by a western hill, near the bay and its bounty, and close to a freshwater spring.

Four generations of David Bakers lived in this house. The carved suns and moons at the sides of the south-facing door match those on another house moved from the island to Cross Street in Wellfleet. They may have been the trademark of the island's master carpenter Stephen Atwood and his young apprentice son Joel, who would have carved them and other specialty trim when commissioned to do so.

The first occupants of this handsome house were Captain David Baker Jr., his wife Debora, their daughter, and their son David and his wife. By 1800, David III's first two children had been born, so seven people from three generations lived in the house in its earliest years.

I noted earlier an inclination for islanders to hypothesize that a house is

---

* The tragic loss of children is logged in town records; children died of measles, croup, scarlet fever, diphtheria, and other diseases, and they were stillborn. In reviewing town records, I discovered entries relating to the Freedman family—in less than a month in spring 1859 they lost a son and four daughters, ages 5 to 15, to scarlet fever.

The Captain David Baker House, c. 1795, now the Baker-Biddle House, with shingled exterior. Originally, this south side was faced in traditional clapboard. 2019

Front door detail of carved crescent moons and suns. Note the series of dentils—tooth-like detailing of small blocks of wood under the roofline—and the "five lights" above the door. Photo courtesy of the *Cape Cod Times*/Steve Heaslip

older than it proves to be. So too with the Baker house, which I heard from one of its last owners was built in the "early 1790s or before." An expert dated the nails used in the construction of the house to approximately 1795. Prior to 1795 all nails were hand-wrought, but those in the Baker house are not.

The Baker men were mariners, but they engaged in several other productive activities. Like most families, the Bakers farmed their land—in their case, the fertile meadowland south of the house and the arable flatland to the north. On their hill to the west stood a grist mill with sails, where they and their neighbors could grind their grains to flour. They also harvested salt meadow grass (or hay) to feed and bed their few animals. The harvest, cut in August and September and stacked in platforms called staddles, was left to freeze in winter. The staddles were then dragged away by horses outfitted with iron shoes with special cleats for traction across the icy marsh.

In 1830, David Baker III, Bound Brook mariner Henry Atwood, and five other men incorporated the Duck Harbor & Beach Company "for the purpose of constructing and keeping in repair such fences, hedges and other works, as may be necessary for the preservation and improvement of the harbour and landing place, which have been formed on the west side of Griffin's Island, in the town of Wellfleet." The company could exact fees from any boat wintering on the beach, at the dock, or at any landing place in Duck Harbor, but it could not exact a fee for merchandise or lumber unloaded there. The existence of this company and its activities highlights the importance of Duck Harbor to all of Wellfleet, not just Bound Brook Islanders.

By the 1840s, the Baker family had also embarked on the manufacture of salt—a necessary commodity for the preservation of fish aboard ships that were on months-long journeys at sea.

Two saltworks operations were erected on Bound Brook Island: an enterprise in the north built by joint owners, and a second built by the Baker family southwest of their house. Why was the manufacture of salt so important? At the time of the American Revolution, the British had been taxing salt imported to the colonies from Liverpool. They eventually imposed an embargo on all shipping, at which time no salt could be imported. Besides preserving fish, one of the Cape's largest exports and its main source of income, salt was critical for preserving food in households. Perhaps responding to the Continental Congress's bounty for domestic salt production, John Sears in nearby Dennis created the first saltworks in the late 1770s and made improvements to his invention for the next 20 years.

By 1800 every town on Cape Cod had saltworks, and by 1837 they numbered 658, producing 26,000 tons of salt a year. Some were large industrial operations, but the Bakers' was a family affair. Everyone, adults and children, pitched in, covering the vats with shallow roofs if rain was arriving, raking salt, and gathering the salt to be stored and dried.

The saltworks were a series of vats within which the rays of the sun evaporated sea water. The vats, made of soft pine imported from Maine, were usually 12 to 20 feet square, 9 to 12 inches deep, and situated about 2 feet above the ground on pilings. The vats were lined up next to each other—you see long lines of them on maps such as the 1848 US Coast Guard Survey. The Bakers' saltworks are visible at the lower left of the map of Bound Brook Island on page 71.

Seawater from the bay was pumped by small windmills from a location just above the high-water mark, through troughs, into the series of vats. The vats had shallow roofs, described by Henry David Thoreau as "turtle-like," which the Bakers used when they needed to protect the saltworks from rain.

Extensive saltworks on Cape Cod

Transformation from seawater to sea salt took about three weeks. Three hundred and fifty gallons of seawater made one bushel of salt that weighed 80 pounds. The saltworks season ran from March through October, taking advantage of the year's strongest rays of sun.

A fishing vessel needed about 700 bushels of salt per year to preserve its catch. The Bakers were providing themselves with a staple essential for their maritime activities. I have not been able to determine when their saltworks were constructed, but they are a feature on the 1848 US Coastal Survey map as well as Walling's 1858 map and Dr. Hopkins's 1860 memory map shown on page 36. The location of Bakers' saltworks suggests that bay waters of Duck Harbor's estuary once came close to the Baker house.

By 1860 the availability of inexpensive domestic and foreign salt was leading to the demise of the salt industry all over the Cape, and at some point the Baker family dismantled the vats, troughs, and small windmills. No sign of them remains today.

The everyday reality for the island community was that subsistence farming, salt manufacturing, hay harvesting, and local maritime activities occupied most of the able men. Although seamen did go on months-long mackerel journeys in fishing season, the rest of the year they gathered shellfish, fished just off the coast, harvested oil from pilot whales they drove to shore, and piloted and ferried cargo and people from shore to shore. They lived by the rhythm of the tides. At their houses, the sun slanting through the south parlor windows told them the hour. Island women spent their days baking bread, preparing meals, farming, putting by fruits and vegetables, and making, laundering, and mending clothing. They tended to the young and old. Families devoted entire Sundays to walking, riding, or boating to the Methodist church service in the town of Wellfleet or Truro.

David Baker III, born in the family house in 1798, married Reuben Rich's daughter Thankful and raised eight children with her. Their third son, Lorenzo Lewis Baker, born in 1832, lived only three years. In 1840 another son was born; he turned out to be their last child together, and they named him Lorenzo as well—Lorenzo Dow Baker. I've seen this often in the Wellfleet birth records: giving a later child the same name as one who had died.

Two years after Thankful Baker's death in 1846, Captain Baker remarried and had one more child, Walter Smith Baker. In Chapter 12, we'll take another look at the later history of the Baker house, which ultimately was taken over by the National Park Service and is now named the Baker-Biddle House.

Two different Bound Brook stories arise from the child named Lorenzo Dow Baker. First, his very name leads us to the account of the Methodist religion on the island. Second, this man was to have a profound influence on thousands of people, and he became, arguably, the most famous citizen of Bound Brook Island and Wellfleet.

5

Methodist Camp Meetings,
1823–1825

BOTH BAKER SONS HAD BEEN NAMED LORENZO to honor a remarkable man who stamped many lives with his religious fervor. This man was the itinerant Methodist evangelist Lorenzo Dow, whom David and Thankful Baker heard preach on Bound Brook Island in the early 1820s. Dow arrived after the earliest years of Methodism had profoundly affected many Cape Cod towns, including Wellfleet.

The Spread of Methodism

A history of the Methodist Church in Wellfleet records that in 1816 several people were "born of the spirit"—including Thomas Atwood, Joel Atwood, and Uriah Atwood, all of whom lived on Bound Brook Island. "Brother Joel Atwood was so full of love, that one day, some little time after his conversion, while at work on the roof of a house, he was heard by the neighbors to shout, 'Glory to God! Glory to God' and then he would sing one of the good old hymns." By 1820, this history continues, the work "has spread to all parts of the town, even to the isles of the sea. On one island [Bound Brook] scarcely an adult is left unconverted and not a single family but some of which have found a pardoning God."

The Methodist movement derived its doctrine of practice and belief from the life and teachings of John Wesley of England. In the United States, Methodism was brought by circuit-riding preachers who visited villages, towns, and cities throughout the southeast and northeast in the early nineteenth century. They preached that salvation was possible for all, not only for a select few as in Calvinism, and for that reason Methodism appealed to entire communities.

The summer camp meetings in the open air were looked forward to all year long. From 1819 through 1822, camp meetings held in South Wellfleet in August drew many hundreds from near and far for five days of outdoor preaching, prayer, singing, visiting, and feasting—the gatherings did not include alcohol, as Methodists were committed to teetotalism.

Camp Meetings on Bound Brook Island

In its August 24, 1824, issue, *Zion's Herald*, the Methodist weekly newspaper published in Boston, announced: "Three packets, full of passengers, sailed from Long-Wharf [in Boston], on Sunday evening, for the Camp meeting at Wellfleet, which commenced yesterday." These packet boats full of passengers with tents and supplies were headed not for South Wellfleet but for Bound Brook Island. The island hosted camp meetings for three years—1823, 1824, and 1825—at the time of the full August moon, taking advantage of the warm summer days and moonlit nights.

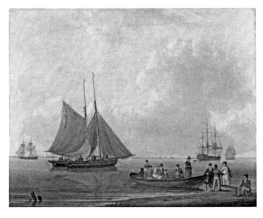

A Wherry Taking Passengers out to Two Anchored Packets, 1825, by William Anderson. Courtesy of the Yale Center for British Art, Paul Mellon Collection

No one knows where on the island the hundreds of souls gathered. Today some suspect the campsite might have overlooked the bay, in the spot where Wellfleetians often picnicked before the Jencks family built a house there in the late 1930s. However, traditionally, campsites for meetings were deliberately chosen without a view so that congregants, enclosed by woods, would focus their attention on the speaker's platform and the passionate oratory about sin and salvation. Perhaps such an enclosed setting was available on that acreage. Certainly, a cart path led from Duck Harbor northward to that area, a freshwater spring was not far away, and ample fishing and shellfish harvesting were available close by.

Henry David Thoreau described the five-day religious gatherings as a singular combination of "a prayer meeting and a picnic." For an isolated community such as Bound Brook, such gatherings must have been momentous.

Disembarking from the packet boats on the shore of Duck Harbor, the travelers went by foot and wagon to the campsite, where they joined Bound Brook families and pitched their tents in a grove of trees. Each tent had its

Early nineteenth-century camp meeting. From an anonymous engraving in Elmer Clark's An Album of Methodist History

own fire and cooking tripod on the outer periphery; clams, oysters, and mussels were eaten in great quantity. The men created an outdoor semicircular amphitheater; they set planks on logs for seating that faced a tall, central preaching platform.

Distinguished Preachers

Preachers from New England and beyond held forth three times a day: at 10 a.m., 3 p.m., and 7 p.m. A man or boy sounded a trumpet to announce the time for assembly. The preaching could be rousing, exhortatory, or inflammatory. Men and women "feeling the spirit" approached the cleared area near the speaker's platform; sometimes they howled, cried, prayed in full voice, or prostrated themselves. Through the preaching, praying, and singing, unawakened souls were brought to Christ, backsliders were reclaimed, and believers were "renewed in love."

Several of the preachers who inspired the souls on Bound Brook Island were of great renown. One was Edward Taylor, later known as Father Taylor, who in 1829 became the chaplain of Boston's Seamen's Bethel, a mission to sailors. The notables who heard Taylor preach in his heyday included Charles Dickens, Herman Melville, Ralph Waldo Emerson—and Walt Whitman, who said of Taylor, "I have never heard but one essentially perfect orator." Indeed, Father Taylor is said to have influenced Whitman's style of writing.

The eccentric itinerant evangelist Lorenzo Dow was perhaps the most famed preacher who held Bound Brook listeners spellbound. Through Father Taylor's notes, we know Lorenzo Dow preached on Bound Brook. Dow owned only one suit, and his hair and beard flowed unkempt. He walked or rode horseback on a circuit through most of what was then the United States. Early in his days on the circuit, he would promise to return to a specific outdoor venue in one year's time and could be relied upon to appear just when promised. Dow also traveled to Ireland and England to preach in open-air assemblies, some of which numbered 10,000 people or more. His autobiography, *The Life and Travels of Lorenzo Dow, Written by Himself: In Which Are Contained Some Singular Providences of God*, was a bestseller in its time, second in sales only to the Bible. The charismatic Dow enthralled his listeners—he shouted, cried, screamed, begged, flattered, insulted his listeners, and challenged their beliefs. He told stories and made jokes.

Dow so impressed the faithful that after hearing him, many families named a son in his honor. The younger brother of the religious leader Brigham Young, who was named Lorenzo Dow Young, accompanied Brigham west to establish the Mormon church in Utah. The Young brothers were born in Smyrna, New York, in one of the earliest circuits young evangelist Lorenzo Dow walked. By the time of the 1850 US Census, Lorenzo had become one of the most popular first names in the United States. As mentioned earlier, Captain David Baker and his wife Thankful heard Lorenzo Dow preach and named not one, but two sons after this unforgettable avatar. The first, Lorenzo Lewis Baker, survived only three years . . . and the second embedded the avatar's full name: Lorenzo Dow Baker.

Lorenzo Dow preaching in the open air

BOUND BROOK CAMP MEETINGS, 1823-5

Where did the faithful,
the hopeful in hundreds
gather those long-ago Augusts?

Where did they pitch tents,
eat, sleep, sing, pray?
No diary, no letter tells.

They circled tents in a grove
near a stream they named
the River Jordan.

Lanterns glowed evenings,
mussels steamed in iron pots,
bedding lay on heaps of straw.

A trumpet summoned them
to hear preacher after preacher
thunder like prophets.

The saved fell
to their knees,
faces shining with tears.

For three summers
spirit lit like fire. The island
absorbed it all.

Lewis Bates, who preached on Bound Brook in 1825 (he might have inspired the choice of middle name of Lorenzo Lewis Baker), wrote enthusiastically about the camp meeting in *Zion's Herald*. As in other reports of camp meetings, Bates's language is florid and abstract; I wish he had added a realistic description of the campsite and the participants. "The fruits of the Camp-meeting are yet visible amongst us, and I have no doubt but that they will be seen in heaven, in the salvation of souls, that will shine before the sapphire throne of God, like refulgent lamps of glory for ever and ever." Amen.

In 1826 the Outer Cape camp meeting was moved to Truro, just north of the island. According to historian Shebnah Rich, the abolitionist and poet Benjamin Drew wrote of that meeting,

> We saw great gatherings in a grove,
> A grove near Pamet Bay,
> Where thousands heard the preached word
> And dozens knelt to pray.

In this poem fragment, consider the number gathered at the assembly: "thousands." It's hard to imagine that many folk arriving on Bound Brook Island in each of the three previous years, but perhaps they did and mysteriously left no trace.

6

Lorenzo Dow Baker

LORENZO DOW BAKER, like his father and grandfathers, was a mariner. Or rather, he began his career as a mariner. His mother died when he was six; by the time he was eight his father had remarried. By the age of ten, in the summer of 1850, "Dow," as he was called, was crewing as a cabin boy, cutting bait and cooking on a mackerel fishing boat on the Newfoundland Banks. In the winter months he walked 10 minutes to the new island school, located on a hill east of the family homestead. Reading Bowditch's *American Practical Navigator* and practicing with a sextant, Dow began his journey to mastery of the seas.

A Wellfleet schoolhouse, undated photo. Children on Bound Brook Island attended a one-room schoolhouse like this one. The island school had a belfry. WHSM

At age 19, Dow traveled by ship and rail to study for a term at Wesleyan Academy in western Massachusetts, a Methodist boarding school now called the Wilbraham and Monson Academy. He returned home in springtime, when the school shut down due to an epidemic of scarlet fever. Though he attended for only one term, this educational experience made an impression on him.

By age 21 Dow was a full-fledged skipper. In that year, 1861, he married Martha Hopkins, his 17-year-old sweetheart, who had also been raised on Bound Brook. Cornelius Hamblin, Martha's generous and wealthy grandfather, gave the newlyweds a house called The Homestead, near Hamblin Farm in Wellfleet. By 1863 the first of their four children was born. Fishing was Dow's livelihood. However, it was sailing—not fishing—that was his true passion.

At 25, Dow Baker bought the *Vineyard*, a small, old fishing vessel. Two years later he traded her in and bought an aging, two-masted 70-ton burden schooner, *Telegraph of Wellfleet*; he put down half the purchase price and mortgaged the remainder. In summer and fall the *Telegraph*, with its Cape Cod crew, fished off the Grand Banks of Maine, and in winter they fished for mackerel south of Cape Hatteras.

Lorenzo Dow Baker in his twenties.
Photo courtesy of William Brewster
Nickerson Cape Cod History Archives
at Cape Cod Community College

To the Tropics, Importing Bananas

Lorenzo Dow Baker dreamed of more than fishing: He imagined trading. He wanted to load aboard his ship all manner of cargo, which he would sell for good profit in a faraway location; he would then load products from that faraway place to sell back in New England. In 1870, when Dow was 30, he took a commission, his first to the tropics, to transport mining equipment 300 miles upriver on the Orinoco in Venezuela. After successful delivery of the equipment, Dow expected to fill the *Telegraph*'s hold with cargo from Venezuela for the ship's return journey, but this did not happen. Dow sailed to Jamaica to make ship repairs and hoped to find cargo there.

In Port Antonio, Jamaica, after the repairs, Baker loaded a cargo of bamboo. But during the week in which repairs were being made, he was introduced to bananas. The next year he returned to Jamaica with goods wanted there— lumber, colorful cloth, dried meat, and fish—and loaded cargo, including bananas and coconuts, for the return voyage. That was the launch of Lorenzo Dow Baker's career as a merchant captain and entrepreneur. Within a few years he created a market for bananas in the northeast United States.

Early on in Dow's life, he evidenced ambition and willingness to take on risk—for example, his purchase of two ships and his daring to venture to South America, where he had never sailed before. For the rest of the 1870s Baker continued to fish for mackerel, with Wellfleet as his base, but increasingly he undertook voyages that delivered raw materials and finished goods to Jamaica and returned to New England with cargoes of ripening bananas.

Founding a Business

At first, Dow bought bananas from local small growers; he then developed the idea of large-scale farming of bananas, which would necessitate creating all the systems needed to bring a large, weather-sensitive crop to distant markets. Jamaica had suffered from the decline of the sugar industry, and the cultivation of bananas revived its economy. Dow became the prime architect of the systems needed for this large-scale agricultural operation: harvest by many hands, cartage by donkey, transport by narrow-gauge railway or skiffs, loading onto ships, purchasing and leasing a fleet (first powered by wind, later by steam), and setting up systems of communication and bookkeeping.

In the 1880s, Baker's dream of a ship as a sort of mobile store had come to fruition. His ships were always full. He and his family began to live most of the year in Jamaica. Looking at today's map of the area around Port Antonio, Jamaica, I discovered a major road named Boundbrook Road and indeed, a banana plantation named Boundbrook. Baker and his family returned in the summer months to Wellfleet. There, they lived at Belvernon, a large house on several acres in town that Dow purchased. A bunch of bananas always hung on Belvernon's front porch for neighbors and passersby to enjoy.

Dow's brother-in-law, Captain Elisha Hopkins of Bound Brook Island, became a partner in the L.D. Baker Company, formed in 1881, and he was important in the Boston administration of the company. Ultimately, Lorenzo Dow

The accounting office of the L.D. Baker Company, staffed by native Jamaicans and men from Wellfleet. WHSM Photo copyright: Thomas Hopkins Baker

Baker took on more partners, and in 1885 the L.D. Baker Company became the Boston Fruit Company.

Over time, many other Wellfleet men found work in Dow's enterprises, including Captain Elisha Rich Atwood, who attended the island school with Dow when they were boys. Captain Atwood worked as a pilot and supercargo and wharf superintendent in Port Antonio, Jamaica.

In his early business years, Dow realized he needed infrastructure in Port Antonio to support his growing enterprise. He constructed a carpentry facility for ship and boat repairs, dormitories for employees, a hospital, a recreational park, a warehouse, and a small hotel for visiting business partners. In later years he donated funds for schools and small churches in Jamaica. He was a devout Methodist who still attended the camp meeting on Cape Cod every August; the *Telegraph*—and, later, the large, purpose-built steamship *L.D. Baker*—had a chapel aboard, including an organ. Lorenzo Dow Baker believed that his good fortune was a gift from God and that he was responsible for his employees and owed them fair wages, proper tools, and good working conditions.

For all the time and energy he devoted to operations in Jamaica, Wellfleet was never far from Baker's heart. As mentioned earlier, he and his family returned each summer and visited with the Baker and Hopkins families; he attended the Methodist camp meetings in Yarmouth, where attendees arrived by railroad from Boston and other towns. When the Methodist church on Main Street in Wellfleet, not far from Belvernon, burned in 1891, Baker contributed funds for its reconstruction.

Dow's father David Baker died at age 84 in 1882. Captain Richard Freeman bought the Baker homestead on Bound Brook Island from the estate for $125. Six months later, Dow bought the homestead back for $214. He then proceeded, over the next two decades and in many transactions, to buy up a good deal of Bound Brook Island. This explains why once, when I was hiking the high spine of the island on the trace of the old cart path, I came across a four-by-four-inch cement stub popping up five inches from the moss; engraved on the top were the initials LDB. This marker was far afield from what I knew to be the bounds of the Baker homestead; Dow was fastidious in marking his holdings all over the island.

Developing Tourism: The Chequesset Inn and Other Ventures

Dow imagined the possibilities for tourism for his hometown, which by the 1880s and 1890s was in an economic downturn as the mackerel catch waned. If the railroad transported many out-of-towners to Yarmouth for camp meetings, he speculated, it could easily transport visitors to Wellfleet as well, to enjoy summer leisure and boating.

In 1885 he purchased Mercantile Wharf, located near Mayo Beach and the heart of Wellfleet. For decades, mackerel had been unloaded and salted on the wharf. After a few years Baker disassembled the fishing operations. On the wharf, extending out over the water on pilings, he built the Chequesset Inn.

The inn opened in July 1902 and featured 20 rooms, according to the *Yarmouth Register*. Constructed at the end of a 400-foot wharf, over the Wellfleet Harbor waters, it had the aspect of a ship at dock. Its guests enjoyed freshwater and saltwater fishing, bathing, and boating; billiards; tennis; and three meals a day. They enjoyed no "spirits," however. As a "Bible-back" Methodist, Lorenzo Dow Baker never drank alcohol, nor did he work on Sundays.

By March 1903, the inn had added 17 more guest rooms for the summer season, along with many improvements, including an enlarged dining room, a telephone booth, a gentlemen's smoking room, a steam laundry, and a room for pool and billiards. On the hotel premises Baker supplied working space to the Massachusetts Department of Fisheries Shellfish Laboratory and Quahog Hatchery. Dow Baker was concerned about the ongoing viability of the shellfish industry in Wellfleet. David Belding, using the lab as his base in 1905, studied the shellfish beds of Wellfleet Harbor and contributed research that has led to the sustained aquaculture of the harbor that lasts till this day.

In an earlier tourism venture, Captain Baker had taken advantage of the financial incentives the Jamaican government offered to builders of hotels, which were needed to accommodate visitors to the Jamaica International Exhibition of 1891. He built the Titchfield Hotel in Port Antonio, adding capacity and features as the years went on. After both the Port Antonio resort and the Wellfleet resort were operating, Baker took advantage of their opposite seasons: He shipped his staff at Titchfield off to Chequesset to work from

CHEQUESSET INN AND BEACH, WELLFLEET, MASS.

The Chequesset Inn, built atop Mercantile Wharf in Wellfleet

Chequesset Inn patrons promenading as on a ship's deck.   WHSM

The Titchfield Hotel, Port Antonio, Jamaica

May through September. In 1905 the Titchfield was rebuilt as a handsome, 400-room hotel, at the time the largest resort in the Americas. Baker's steamships began to carry tourists south to Jamaica for their holidays and then load up with bananas and returning tourists for the journey back north.

Baker explored many other business ventures. He purchased Corn Hill in Truro, where the *Mayflower* men had found the Pamets' store of corn in 1620, with the idea of turning it into a national monument. He built rental cottages at Millennium Grove, where the Yarmouth camp meetings took place. He owned shares in a fleet of 15 coal schooners. He owned and became president of the profitable steamship company that plied the route from Plymouth to Boston.

The United Fruit Company

Boston Fruit's enterprises grew. By 1895 the company owned 40,000 acres in Jamaica, including 35 plantations and deep-water frontage in the harbors of Port Antonio and Port Morant. Growth—through diversified geography of production and markets, with faster shipping via steam—seemed to be the insurance needed to counteract the unpredictable effects of weather on crops and ocean transport. To become even larger and stronger, Boston Fruit reorganized into the United Fruit Company in 1899.

Lorenzo Dow Baker did not support the company's expansion of the business beyond Jamaica to countries such as Costa Rica and Honduras. He relinquished his top executive post and remained in Jamaica as tropical manager. Some saw his stand as principled; others judged that he was too old-fashioned for the new corporate imperatives. In any case, Baker was not part of the rapacious growth of the fruit business, the bribery and corruption that led to the term "banana republic."

Philanthropy

Bananas made Lorenzo Dow Baker wealthy, and he was generous with his wealth, which he believed came from God. He sent many Jamaican boys, and eventually girls, to New England: those who were sick for medical treatment and others for education, which he strongly supported due to his experience at Wesleyan Academy. Although he helped to finance both causes, he told the youths he wanted them to pay him his money back—but to take their time. When his nephew John L. Hopkins, a theological student aiming to be a missionary, died, Dow was the major donor for the John L. Hopkins Memorial Eye Hospital in Peking (now Beijing), founded by John's Methodist missionary brother Dr. Nehemiah Somes Hopkins. Dow was also a major benefactor of the First Methodist Church of Boston, with annual gifts of $25,000. In Wellfleet, he refurbished at least 20 abandoned houses, which then were rented to out-of-town visitors. He paid the real estate taxes on the houses of neighbors who were having a hard time.

In 1905 Captain Baker was honored in Jamaica for his many contributions to the island and showered with gifts and tributes. At the Wellfleet Historical Society, which has devoted several rooms to him, you can view a photograph of Dow at the celebration. He is surrounded by well-wishers and many items of silver, including an elaborate tea set. On this occasion one official was quoted: "In thirty years Captain Baker has done more for Jamaica than the British Empire in three hundred years."

Support for the Herring River Dike

When he was in his sixties, Lorenzo Dow Baker had the welfare of his own and others' business interests in the burgeoning tourist industry in mind as he became involved in a major effort to rid Wellfleet of mosquitoes. He lent his stature as Wellfleet's most prominent son to this project. In 1906 a commissioned study by Boston civil engineers, who in fact knew little about mosquitoes, endorsed a proposal to dike the Herring River to diminish the mosquito population and create additional land. The Chequesett Country Club and golf course were partially built on this "reclaimed land."

The town of Wellfleet signed on to the dike project, and ground was broken in August 1908—two months after Baker died of heart disease. The dike, completed by 1910, profoundly changed the river and its estuary: It reduced the width of the river's outlet from 400 feet to 6 feet, and the 1,100-acre estuary, the second largest in New England, to 10 acres. It did not solve the mosquito problem. We'll return to the fate of the Herring River, which was so important to Bound Brook Island, in a later chapter.

So ended the life of a successful man of imagination who had exceptional organizational and "people skills," a man of honor and philanthropy. In addition to his business activities, Dow was a trustee of Boston University and other enterprises and a member of many clubs. He raced yachts and was president of the yacht-building firm Baker Yacht Basin in Quincy. Yet he was moderate in his personal life: His two homes, one in Wellfleet and another in Jamaica, were comfortable but in no way opulent—they featured ordinary furniture and candlewick white bedspreads.

In June 1908, Dow, very ill, sailed from Jamaica to Boston to seek medical care. He checked into the Parker House Hotel. A maid discovered him there when he did not reply to any summons.

I was stunned to see his death certificate; the clerk entered L. D. Baker's profession in large, dark letters: "Capitalist." That is correct, of course. Lorenzo Dow Baker was a capitalist. I believe he was a "good" capitalist—a "high" capitalist, we might now say. The cultivation and export of bananas revived the Jamaican economy after sugar plantations went bust. He provided adequate compensation to his employees. He gave substantial amounts of money for worthy causes—in Jamaica, Wellfleet, Boston, and Peking.

The Wellfleet–Jamaica connection continued through time. For decades after L. D. Baker's death, Wellfleet families worked in the Jamaican banana and sugar trades, farmed on large land holdings, and raised their children there. Now we will leave this man of imagination and energy, this capitalist who affected the lives of so many, and move on through time.

7

From Settlement to
Community in 1850

AN EARLY OBSESSION OF MINE WAS THE HUNT FOR MAPS proving
Bound Brook Island was at one time *an island*—because it is not an island in
the present day.

What Maps Told Me

The 1775 map of Cape Cod and Narragansett Bays by Charles Blaskowitz, a
surveyor for England's King George III, was one of many commissioned in
preparation for possible conflict between the crown and the American colonies. This large map—2 feet by 2.5 feet in dimension—impresses with its
remarkable level of detail: Not only did the mapmaker track specifics of a large
coastline, but he also noted each structure on land with a red dot, visible in
close-up in the online version of this beautiful map.

On my computer I easily zoomed in on the image of Bound Brook Island.
I could see, yes, water surrounding the island, with a large harbor to its south.
This map and several other early maps are evidence that the island was not
misnamed. But Blaskowitz documented so much more.

Cape Cod and Narragansett Bays, in a 1775 map by Blaskowitz.
Courtesy of the Library of Congress

Enlargement of Blaskowitz's 1775 map showing Bound Brook Island at left

The seven dots on Blaskowitz's Bound Brook Island represent the earliest evidence of habitation by European settlers: two in the north (overlapping one another—one of them I believe is Reuben Rich's homestead), one mid-island, and four in the south. One of those in the south assuredly was Thomas Higgins's house, built in 1730. But no records I've found name the owners of the other structures.

Other Records of Early Settlement

The first federal census in 1790 did not distinguish Bound Brook Island inhabitants from those of the rest of Wellfleet. The closest we may come to determining its inhabitants at the turn of the eighteenth century is aided by the list of ten men including Reuben Rich, who petitioned the town to allow them to lay out new roads on Bound Brook Island in 1800 and 1801. By surname they are Rich (Reuben, Elisha, Isaac), Atwood (Eleazer, Freeman, Thomas, Stephen, Richard, Isaiah), and Higgins (Solomon). Why David Baker, whose house we know was built by 1800, did not take part in the laying out of roads near his house is unknown—perhaps none of the new "ways" impinged on his lands. Records show that the town compensated landowners who gave up land for the new roads. We can assume that by 1800 at least 11 inhabited houses dotted the island: the 10 road-makers' and Captain Baker's.

Enough young growing families had settled on the island in the following decades that a school was built. We know this because the *History of the Methodist Episcopal Church in Wellfleet* records that one of three Sabbath schools, established in 1827 in Wellfleet, was held "at the Island school house." The Sabbath school superintendant was Uriah Atwood, who lived on the east end of the island. Well documented is the successor school building, inaugurated in 1844. It was probably constructed on the same hilltop site, near the houses of Thomas Atwood and Samuel Bunting and the island's main road.

The 1848 Map that Revealed the Island's Community

By far the most exciting map for me is the "US Coast Guard Survey Map of Billingsgate to the Pamet River" of 1848. It maps, with exacting detail, not only topography but settlement. Using my computer, I was again able to zoom in on the digital version to focus on Bound Brook Island.

Suddenly before me was a map of a community. I could see not only dwellings, barns, outbuildings, the schoolhouse, and cart paths but also orchards, saltworks, marshes, pasture fences, and elevations. I have studied the map so often that now it is more familiar to me than the palm of my hand. A legend to this map's topographic symbols appears on page 162.

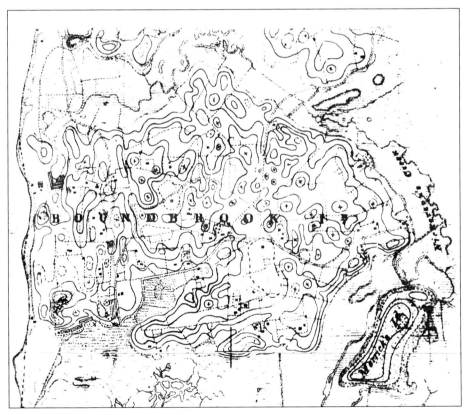

Bound Brook Island, detail from US Coast Guard Survey map, 1848

Matching the Map with the Census

This detailed map of Bound Brook Island in 1848, together with the first detailed census taken only two years later, gave me a way to begin to understand the community that had formed on the island. The 1850 US Census provided me with a way to assign families to the houses shown on the 1848 map.* Ten years earlier, the US Census listed Wellfleet's population, including Bound Brook Island's, alphabetically by last name of the householder. That made it impossible to determine which householders lived on the island.

Matching houses with the families that inhabited them was possible for the first time with information available in 1850. Census taker Isaiah Gifford, arriving by boat, docked at Duck Harbor. He began his list in the south part of the island with Captain Samuel Rich's homestead and proceeded, dwelling by dwelling, in a rough zigzag circle counterclockwise. He finished with Rebecca Rich's, one of a cluster of houses in the northwest. I could figure this out because I knew—for certain, from real estate records and other documents—who inhabited 14 of the houses scattered over the island. The remaining 12 assignments of families to houses are my best guesses, relying on subsequent maps and Gifford's walking pattern. On September 7, 1850, Gifford surveyed 26 households.

Tracing Family Connections with the 1850 Census

The 1850 US Census collected much more information than any previous census. Earlier censuses simply listed the householder's name, with tick marks for the others in the household by categories such as gender, age range, and race. But the 1850 US Census, for the first time, names each person in the household, along with age, gender, race, and birthplace, and the occupation of males over 15; value of real estate; with a final column to note anyone who was "deaf and dumb, blind, idiot, pauper or convict." (No one on Bound Brook Island was marked in this last column.) For the first time we are able to see the names

---

* The 1850 US Census of households on Bound Brook Island is reproduced on pages 156–160.

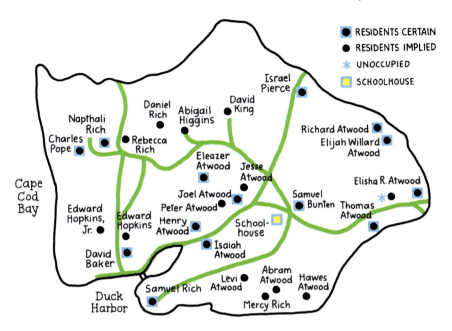

RESIDENTS CERTAIN
RESIDENTS IMPLIED
UNOCCUPIED
SCHOOLHOUSE

Israel
Pierce

David
King

Daniel
Rich

Abigail
Higgins

Napthali
Rich

Richard Atwood

Charles
Pope

Rebecca
Rich

Elijah Willard
Atwood

Eleazer
Atwood

Jesse
Atwood

Cape
Cod
Bay

Elisha R. Atwood

Joel Atwood

Samuel
Bunten

Peter Atwood

Edward
Hopkins,
Jr.

Edward
Hopkins

Henry
Atwood

Thomas
Atwood

School-
house

David
Baker

Isaiah
Atwood

Abram
Atwood

Hawes
Atwood

Levi
Atwood

Samuel Rich

Duck
Harbor

Mercy Rich

Bound Brook Island houses in 1848, labeled with householders'
names retrieved from the 1850 US Census

of the wives and mothers and the names of children and other relatives in a
household.

Many Atwoods headed households, as well as many Riches. How were
they related? Because all family members were listed, I could look at the inter-
connectedness of families. For example, seeing the names of wives for the first
time I could research who they were; I often discovered they were daughters
and granddaughters of original settlers. I used the ancestry.com website as a
genealogical resource to research who was related to whom.

I drew my own large map on a huge easel pad, locating the 26 houses and
labeling them with family names, following Isaiah Gifford's path as he walked
the entire island. Ultimately, through the census and my research on family ge-
nealogies, I began to see the extent of family ties that characterized the Bound
Brook community in 1850.

I used a blue marker to draw lines connecting all the houses where sons
of Richard Atwood lived: six houses, housing seven brothers. Yes, two adult
brothers lived in the same house. This is a hallmark of life in the 1700s and

1800s: Sometimes two related families shared a single house. In 1850 on Bound Brook Island, 30 families lived in 26 houses.

The island was essentially populated by the descendants of Atwoods and Richs—likely because they had laid claim to the greater portions of the island originally, and they could give acreage to their offspring. The Baker and Hopkins families, with smaller footholds, did not proliferate in this same fashion, though there were marriages between the two families and between other island families.

The heads of 13 households were Atwood men, all related as brothers or cousins. Their sisters, daughters, and cousins had married householders Edward Hopkins Sr., David King, and Daniel Rich, and thus 20 of 26 houses were inhabited by Atwood male and female descendants.

Five houses are headed by Riches (including Daniel, counted above) and Samuel Bunten, who married Sally Rich of the Riches of neighboring Truro. Israel Pierce was a Rich—his grandfather Elisha Rich and his grandfather's brother Reuben laid out Bound Brook Island cart roads in 1800, and his wife was a descendant of Thomas Higgins, who built the first house on Bound Brook in 1730. One house, owned by the Hopkins family, was rented out to a couple unrelated to anyone else on the island; their story will be told in the next chapter.

Many more Atwoods and Riches lived in the town of Wellfleet and on Griffin's Island. In fact, you will find those family names all over Cape Cod. The idea intrigues me, though, that for a while so many brothers, so many interconnected relatives, lived within walking distance of one another on Bound Brook Island. That proximity is foreign to me, my own family being so far flung: New Hampshire; Rhode Island; New York State; Washington, DC; Virginia; Tennessee; California. On Bound Brook in 1850, seven brothers lived within walking distance of one another, some only a stone's throw away, plus cousins, uncles, daughters-in-law, sons, fathers, mothers, and grandchildren. The whirl of Atwoods and Riches is dizzying. It was as if in 1850 Bound Brook Island was not only a community, it was also one family—a family that was, however, just beginning to disperse.

As evidenced in the maps and censuses of other years, houses changed owners and children inherited from parents; the Barnstable County Registry of Deeds records hundreds of transactions of deeds and wills involving houses as well as uplands and salt meadows. Before and after 1850, these and other families lived on Bound Brook Island: Higgins, Wiley, Hopkins, Lombard, Young, Knowles, Mayo, Curran, Cobb.

On Bound Brook Island in the year 1850 resided a community of remarkable closeness, of almost unbelievably tight family ties. What was it like when those ties began to unwind, when family after family left the island, some for the town of Wellfleet, some migrating far beyond?

8

Two Stories from 1850:
E. L. Atwood and the Pope Family

THE HOUSE OWNED IN OUR TIME by my neighbor Jack Hall, later by his family, had been inhabited by Henry Atwood, one of seven sons of Richard Atwood. Henry lived in that house from at least 1830 until his death in 1874.

According to Jack Hall, in the 1830s Henry Atwood built—across the cart path from his house—the three-quarter Cape house my family now occupies in summertime, called the Ebenezer L. Atwood House. In the keeping room the original wood wainscoting is in place. On the second floor the unpainted floorboards in the bedroom are 19 inches wide, testament to the few remaining large fir trees that once grew on the island, where we now mostly see skinny pitch pine, scrub oak, and lanky locusts.

An Atwood Leaves the Island

Jack told me the house was a wedding gift from Henry to his firstborn son Ebenezer Atwood and his daughter-in-law Margaret Crosby. This is a charming story, but is it true? The 1850 census shows that Ebenezer and Margaret, married in 1843, were not living on Bound Brook Island. A mariner, Ebenezer

The Joel Atwood House: Generations of the Henry Atwood family owned it from 1830 to 1929. 2020

The Ebenezer L. Atwood House, c. 1830s, a three-quarter Cape, with an addition on the right side. 2020

was living in the town of Wellfleet, two doors away from his in-laws, and censuses reveal that his uncle Isaiah Atwood's family occupied the Bound Brook house opposite Henry Atwood's house for decades. County records show that Henry Atwood owned this house until his death, and in 1879 his heirs—Ebenezer's siblings Mulford, Mary, and Elisha—sold their shares of the house for 50 dollars to Ebenezer's wife Clara. Evidently, Ebenezer had inherited a share, along with each of his siblings.

Ebenezer Atwood was emblematic: Born on the island, he decided to make a life elsewhere. His choice was a harbinger of the depopulation of Bound Brook Island, a slow exiting of family after family over the next 40 years. Perhaps Ebenezer found life on the island too inbred or perhaps he was prescient, foreseeing the maritime access of Duck Harbor silting up.

In late 1850 Ebenezer's wife Margaret died soon after childbirth, making him a 30-year-old widowed mariner with two small daughters. He left Wellfleet and moved to the Boston area, where he launched a successful career as a tea merchant, remarried, and ultimately sired seven more children.

"E. L. Atwood Esq.," read the *Yarmouth Register* in 1889, "was in town getting his summer residence on Bound Brook Island ready for occupancy." Through the mid-1890s Ebenezer Atwood came from his home in Somerville near Boston to his Wellfleet "cottage" in the summer, often accompanied by his daughter Clara Isabel. Ebenezer and his daughter may have been Bound Brook Island's first "summer people."

In 1903 the Ebenezer Atwoods deeded the Bound Brook house to their youngest son, Arthur, born in 1873. Arthur Atwood lived there in the summertime in the late teens and '20s of the twentieth century. To my knowledge, Arthur was the last Atwood to live on Bound Brook Island. He died there in 1929 and was buried in Wellfleet.

Years ago, I was washing the small panes of old glass in a "six and nine" window of the Ebenezer L. Atwood house, a window that looks out onto our wide yard, facing the cart path. As I wiped a pane, the past appeared.

ETCHED

Only now have I seen it,
as I've come, damp cloth in hand,
to claim this antique house
by cleaning. I rub
the dimpled glass
and *25 of May* appears
etched in morning light.
And an *H*, like a ribbon
beginning *Henry*.

Someone loved this house
and this land, and is gone
with his stories.
Remember this pane of glass
I say to my six-year son.
I wipe it shiny, looking through
to the century-old mulberry tree
he runs out to climb.

I had wondered why the glass pane had been etched with *H* for *Henry*, when his brother Isaiah had lived in this house for decades. The answer relates to the fact that wood and glass were precious, never thrown away. When this small addition to the house was built, perhaps an old window at Henry Atwood's house was pulled out of storage in the barn and brought across the path to be installed. I've tried to find the meaning of *May 25*, but it has disappeared. I can't identify it as someone's birthday or marriage date, but it was a day important enough for *H* to etch in time.

The Popes

Only one family on Bound Brook Island in 1850 was unrelated to anyone else, and their story, at least what we know of it, is of great interest historically and in human terms.

Charles Pope and his wife Sarah, Black Americans, identified in the US Census with a "B," were 24 and 22, respectively in 1850 when they rented the Hopkins homestead, in northwest Bound Brook Island. (The Hopkins family—whose forbears were original settlers of the island—lived off-island from 1845–1855.) According to historian Everett Nye, Charles Pope was "a 'high class' steward on a first class ship." In 1850, Charles and Sarah Pope were listed as the only Black family in all of Wellfleet, among its total population of 2,411.

How is that the Popes came to Bound Brook? Perhaps a seafaring captain—Daniel Rich, whose house is nearby, or Thomas Hopkins—struck up an acquaintance or friendship with Charles Pope. Maybe Pope did something extraordinary on a voyage, putting a Bound Brook seafarer in a debt of gratitude. Or was it something else? Why was Charles Pope looking for a quiet, out-of-the-way place to settle? The Popes were counted in the September 7, 1850, circuit of the island that census-taker Gifford made. The Fugitive Slave Act of 1850 was signed into law on September 18, 1850—certainly, its contents were known and debated long before its passage into law. Whether enslaved or free, Black men and women could be captured by hunters and brought south for enslavement.

Barnstable County deeds show that on October 1853, Charles Pope bought land and a "dwelling house" on the north of the island for $125 from carpenter Joel Atwood. One could surmise that the Popes liked the quiet of the island and decided to make it their permanent home. (The new house was situated on cleared land where Israel Pierce's house had been before being moved into Wellfleet.) However, one year later—in October 1854—Charles Pope sold this property to Nathaniel P. Wiley, a Wellfleet man, for $125. Why?

I went online to see what I could find out. My search turned up a catastrophic event reported on page 3 of the December 1, 1854, issue of William Lloyd Garrison's abolitionist newspaper *The Liberator*, published in Boston.

In late November 1854, two steamboats collided in Boston Harbor, causing an explosive fire and loss of life. The penultimate paragraph of *The Liberator*'s account states: "Mr. Charles Pope, a colored passenger who resides at Cape Cod and follows the fishing business, had his thigh and ribs broken and

Boston Harbor *by Fitz Henry Lane, 1854*

it was thought he would not live through the night. His wife was also severely injured." (See the full *Liberator* article on page 161 at the end of this book.)

The Popes had been passengers on the side-wheel paddle steamboat *Ocean* setting out from Boston for Bath, Maine, on its last passage of the season. What was the purpose of their trip in cold late November? They had sold the house they had only recently purchased. It's likely they were free Blacks, yet their lives were still at risk. Unscrupulous slave catchers roamed Boston and elsewhere, empowered by the Fugitive Slave Act of 1850. Although the harbor town of Bath, Maine, was stridently anti-abolitionist, nearby Portland, 34 miles southwest of Bath, was a station on the Underground Railroad. Could it be that the Popes had decided to make their way to Canada, where their freedom would be assured? Then, just as their journey began, Charles and Sarah Pope had been severely injured.

A half year later, the August 1855 Massachusetts Census records that the Popes were residents of the town of Wellfleet. Had they been recuperating in town, near medical attention and supplies? In November of this same year,

Sarah gave birth to their only child, Charles Jr. The last mention of Charles Sr. that I have found is his name, "C. Pope," on the 1858 Walling map. The name appears at the northern location of the dwelling on Bound Brook Island that he bought and then sold to Nathaniel Wiley. I found no record of a sale back to the Popes in the Barnstable County Registry. In 1855 the town of Wellfleet had three Overseers of the Poor, and Nathaniel P. Wiley—the man to whom the Popes sold their house in 1854—was one of the overseers. Did Wiley rent the house to the Popes?

The 1860 US Census lists only Sarah Pope, 30, and son Charles Pope, 5, in that same house. Sarah is listed as widowed in the 1865 Massachusetts Census. Did Charles Pope Sr. die as a consequence of his injuries from the steamboat collision, or was he later lost at sea? We do not know the end of his story.

For decades, Sarah Pope remained in that house. The 1880 US Census lists her, age 50, and her son Charley Jr., age 24, a sailor. The Popes' story may have involved generosity or charity, but it certainly also involves stoicism, fortitude, and character. How did Sarah support herself without her husband, with no family nearby, raising a child alone? How did she keep her house warm, keep food on the table?

Scraps of the past have come to me about Sarah Pope. Jack Hall said he had been told that Mrs. Pope, as he always called her, drew sand pictures on the floor of the hearth room and that she became a midwife for the island women. It was said that one of the houses closest to hers, Elisha Atwood's, had an extra-large room on the second floor where island women came to give birth—attended, I like to believe, by Sarah Pope. Was she also an herbalist? I imagine her cultivating a large garden.

My only hint on Sarah's origins is her listing in the 1865 state census, which gives Taunton, Massachusetts, as her birthplace. The 1830 US Census for Taunton lists only one Black family, a free family with seven members; there is one tick mark in the column for females under 10, which I presume would be Sarah, born in 1827. Another whole story opens up here. In 1830, the head of that household in Taunton was Peter Adams, 88, a one-time enslaved man, later freed, who served in the Revolutionary War. He lived to the age of 101 on his own homestead. Taunton's historical commission recounted his story on a plaque erected in 1976 in a family cemetery. Sarah's relation to

Peter Adams is unknown. I posit that Sarah was born free. We do not know if her husband, Charles Pope, was also born free, but his many years as a sailor suggest that he was.

Sarah Pope died on September 22, 1881, in her early fifties, of apoplexy—what we today call a stroke. Centuries of Wellfleet death records are fastidious—each death lists the parents of the deceased, but Sarah Pope's were "Unknown." As for what happened to Charles Pope Jr., his trail ran cold.

The lives of many women who lived on Bound Brook Island remain unwritten. The little we know is embedded in the records of births and deaths of many children. What we know about Sarah Pope, though, is more than I have learned about any other woman of her era who lived on Bound Brook Island.

9

The Hopkins Family:
A Story of Tragedy and Survival

THE THOMAS HOPKINS FAMILY has a long history and involvement with Bound Brook Island, from its earliest days of settlement to today. I came to know one of the family's descendants, Joan Hopkins Coughlin. In 1850 the Thomas Hopkins family was not occupying its house on Bound Brook, though the Hopkins family did return to Bound Brook after 1850—for a while.

Mayflower Beginnings

The Hopkinses arrived on the North American continent on the *Mayflower*, preceding the arrivals of Richs and Atwoods. I tracked Giles Hopkins in 1620 to his direct descendent Joan Hopkins Coughlin, whom I can visit at her Golden Cod Gallery in Wellfleet, where she and her husband Jack Coughlin display their artwork. My friendship with Joan links me to the past of Bound Brook Island and the earliest days of Cape settlement. We've enjoyed many hours matching her family stories, notes, and photographs with my research. Joan's family embodied Bound Brook Island's shift from seafaring to other occupations and their relocations from the island to elsewhere.

I met Joan years ago at the Wellfleet Historical Society and learned that her great-grandfather Thomas lived on Bound Brook, and she still goes there to paint the landscape. Her love for the island is deep. I knew early on of her direct *Mayflower* connection, and then I learned that she was born in Jamaica. Her grandfather Richard had been connected with the United Fruit Company, the successor to L. D. Baker's banana enterprises.

The Hopkins family was rooted in the earliest European settlement of New England and pursued a typical marine livelihood, reaching out eventually beyond Cape Cod to other endeavors. My profiles of Reuben Rich and Lorenzo Dow Baker looked at their achievements in the world, but the Thomas Hopkins family has drawn me closer to understanding the harsh realities of the nineteenth century: the world of devastating gales and the wrenching upheavals caused by deaths and catastrophe, including a house burning to the ground.

Loss After Loss

In the late 1700s the Captain Thomas Hopkins family settled in the northwest tip of Bound Brook, just over the town line from Wellfleet and officially lying in Truro. The elder Thomas was lost at sea in 1825 and left his widow Susannah in the house on Bound Brook Island with seven children, one of whom was young Thomas, Joan's great-grandfather. He was born in 1814 on Bound Brook and was 11 years old when his father died at sea.

I think about Thomas's mother Susannah: Widowed at 32, she was left alone on a windswept island to raise seven children: Lucy, 13; Thomas, 11; twins Jerusha and Susannah, 8; Nehemiah, 6; Richard, 3; and Elisha, 1. A father left with this many motherless children could find another wife, but a widow was unlikely to find a man willing to take on the burden of supporting eight souls beside himself. Who was going to support this family of eight?

Family lore has Thomas shipping off to sea to jig mackerel to earn a living for his family when he was 11. I imagine that nearby families—the Reuben Riches and David Bakers of Bound Brook Island and others from South Truro—helped the struggling household.

Eight years later, in January 1833, tragedy struck again when Susannah died at 41. Thomas, then 19, took on the role of head of the family. The three sisters and four brothers stayed together, but by 1836 all three Hopkins sisters had married and made their homes elsewhere, and one brother, Nehemiah, had also left home. Thomas married Hope Hamblin in 1836, and the 1840 US Census for Truro showed that Thomas's household also included his two youngest brothers.

Thomas and Hope had no children in their first five years of marriage, which was unusual for those times. Thomas and his brothers Richard and Elisha, both under 20, were all mariners, out at sea catching mackerel. The usual voyage for mackerel fishing involved five months away from home on the seas. I found a notation to this effect on the 1850 US Census for Industry for Wellfleet. I imagine Hope alone for almost half the year as her husband and his brothers earned their livings, although she may have returned to her large, wealthy family at Hamblin Farm, only a few miles south in Wellfleet, for company when Thomas and his brothers were away.

As if orphanhood were not enough, fire then claimed the Hopkins home, leaving behind only charred timbers and ashes. Truro neighbors led by young carpenter Zacheus Rich built another house for the Hopkins family, just over the town boundary in the Wellfleet part of Bound Brook Island. Thomas promised to repay the neighbors when he could, and a family story says he did just that, "with interest." We do not know when that fire took place, but I believe it must have happened after 1840, because Thomas, his wife Hope, and his two brothers, as noted above, were counted in the 1840 US Census for Truro, not Wellfleet.

Thomas and his growing family may have lived in the new house for a few years sometime after 1840. However, according to county deeds, in 1848 Thomas purchased a home and land near the large Hamblin family estate, where his brother Elisha was living. I believe Elisha had moved there because he married another Hamblin, Hope's younger sister Cordelia. By the time of the 1850 census, Thomas, Hope, and three children were indeed living near the Hamblins in Wellfleet. I think the Hopkinses rented their small Cape house on Bound Brook Island to people outside the family for a number of years (for a few years to a couple, Charles and Sarah Pope). By 1860 the house was inhabited by Hopkins family members again: Thomas's brother Richard and his wife.

At the Fishing Grounds *by Fitz Henry Lane, 1851. Schooners fished for mackerel on Georges Bank, the crew using jigging lines over the rail.*

Sea Captain and Wharf Owner

In the prime of his life, Thomas Hopkins became a successful captain, fishing for mackerel on Georges Bank and in other prime areas. Mackerel fishing had supplanted cod fishing at just around about the time young Thomas went to sea. Boys such as Thomas could lean against a schooner's rail with a jig in their hands and hook mackerel, flipping each almost foot-long fish into a barrel on deck.

Hopkins commanded a series of schooners: *Olio*, *Clarinda*, *Bloomer*, *Emily*, and *Joshua Hamblin*, and he employed five hands year-round. The value of the catch minus the outfitter's charge and the charge for food during the voyage was then divided: 25 percent of the profit went to the vessel's owners, and the crew divided the remainder (skippers received larger shares). Historian Samuel Eliot Morison has the financial records for a four- or five-month voyage in 1843 of the schooner *Boundbrook*, for which a crew member might earn $19 ($694 in 2021 dollars) and a skipper, $54 ($1,974 in 2021 dollars).

In 1845 Thomas joined with seven other mariners, most of whom were Bound Brook men, in ownership of the River Wharf Company. The Company had a wharf on the southern side of Chequessett Neck (Chequessett means "large place" in Algonquin), at the mouth of the Herring River where its waters enter Wellfleet Harbor. River Wharf included a warehouse and a small store selling gear and supplies.*

Crews unloaded hauls of mackerel, salted and packed into barrels, from the fishing vessels onto River Wharf at Chequessett Neck, where they were stored before shipment off-Cape. Thomas Hopkins's haul for the entire year 1850 was 388 barrels (each weighed 200 lb.), valued in total at $2,690 ($94,500 in 2021 dollars). His marine enterprise was fully integrated: fishing for mackerel, warehousing for shipment to market, and supplies for provisioning vessels for the next voyage.

Lumber Dealer in Boston

Thomas Hopkins marked a significant turn in his life when he was around 40 years old. It was 1854, and he decided to go into business in the Boston area with his brother Elisha and brother-in-law Joshua Hamblin, sourcing lumber from Maine and elsewhere for shipment to Cape Cod. Lumber was always in demand on the Cape, which no longer had its own supply due to deforestation. Thomas settled his family in Charlestown, north of Boston.

Why did Thomas make this major life change? Could he have been mindful of, even haunted by, the great hazards of sea life, the many storms that claimed mariners? His father, age 40, had been lost at sea in 1825.

Historian Shebnah Rich devotes an entire chapter of his book *Truro—Cape Cod or Land Marks and Sea Marks* to shipwrecks and loss of life, including the devastating "October Gale" of 1841, which drowned 57 men and boys from Truro who were at sea on Georges Bank, the most westward of the great Atlantic fishing banks. Thomas Hopkins would have been acquainted with many of the mariners who never returned.

---

* The River Wharf Company eventually took over Bound Brook Island's one small, informal general store, which was operated by carpenter Joel Atwood beginning in 1835, probably out of his barn. This store appears on no maps of the island; River Wharf Company likely ran it for only a few years.

LAMENT

One in five who called Wellfleet home
sailed the oceans, whaling, then fishing
for cod, then mackerel: captains, cooks,
mates, cabin boys. Few knew how to swim.
In one Bound Brook Island family
all five males were *Persons Employed*
in Navigation of the Ocean: the narrow
columns of the 1840 Census tell me:
one 10–14 years old, one 15–19,
two 20–29 and one 50–59. No family
was unscathed by loss—cousin, uncle,
brother, father, husband, son.

I stand on a hill overlooking the sea.
Was it here a man, missing two sons,
scanned the horizon with his glass?
Did their mother pack him lunch?
Did he stay each day till the sun set?
How many weeks, or months,
before he lay the scope above
the hearth, on the mantel, for good?

Perhaps Thomas thought working on land would be safer for him and his family. But in April 1856—in the middle of his long life—he suffered another great loss: His wife, Hope, died, leaving him with four young children, ages 13 to 3.

Return to Wellfleet

Seven months later Thomas married Hannah Rich, a 29-year-old spinster (as she would have been described at that time). In contrast to his widowed mother Susannah, who had had no chance of remarrying on account of her

The Thomas Hopkins family occupied the house on the right in the late 1850s. At its left is the Atwood-Higgins House, above the Herring River. Photo facing north, from the early 1900s. WHSM

seven dependents, the widower Thomas, with his stature as a sea captain and businessman, was a substantial catch.

Hannah Rich had grown up in Truro. Her middle name is Hopkins but, oddly, I found no one named Hopkins in her family tree. This leads me to suspect that her father and Thomas's father, Truro seamen, may have been friends when Thomas Hopkins Sr. was lost at sea two years before Hannah's birth. Hannah herself was no stranger to tragedy: When she was 14, her brother Jesse, 18, was one of the 57 Truro mariners lost in the October Gale of 1841.

Where did Thomas and Hannah settle? On Bound Brook Island. Thomas settled into a house slightly northeast up the hill from the Atwood-Higgins house. His name is shown there on the 1858 Walling map of Barnstable County. It's likely the Hopkins homestead in the west of the island was occupied by his brother Richard and his family when Thomas precipitously returned to Wellfleet, remarried, and resumed his maritime vocation.

In November 1857 Hannah Hopkins delivered the first of her four sons. In 1860 her third son, Nehemiah, was born. The same year, Thomas's daughter with his first wife, Hope—Jerusha, age 8—died of measles, a deadly childhood disease in the nineteenth century.

Captain Thomas Hopkins Jr. Photo courtesy of Joan Hopkins Coughlin

Four years later, in 1864, Thomas purchased from his brother Richard's estate the Hopkins homestead, built after the 1840s fire. Thomas moved his family of seven from the east of the island to this house of many memories. Yet he did not plan to stay on Bound Brook Island. It was clear by then that his business future lay where there was a functional harbor. In 1865 he bought a parcel of land in the town of Wellfleet, and by 1870 he had flaked the Bound Brook house and moved it to Baker Avenue.

The second Hopkins homestead, built in the 1840s. This photo was taken shortly before the house was flaked and moved off-island by 1870. Photo courtesy of Joan Hopkins Coughlin

By the 1880s, worn from a life at sea, Captain Thomas Hopkins again went into business with his brother Elisha. Elisha Hopkins, a one-time mariner, had become a lumber dealer in Boston and, finally, a homeopathic physician living in New York State. There, he formulated his own government-patented medicines, called patent medicines, in glass bottles bearing his name. Thomas also began to sell patent medicines from the Nathan Wood Company in Portland, Maine, as reported in the *Barnstable Patriot*. Thomas traveled to Portland and also "out west" as a traveling salesman. The 1880 US Census lists Thomas Hopkins's occupation as "huckster."*

---

* In 1880 the appellation of huckster probably carried a less pejorative meaning than it does today.

Because we've encountered brother Elisha yet again in Thomas's life, I'd like to take a sidestep to write about family names and how they frequently confounded me as I've worked with generations of Bound Brook families. This was especially true of the Hopkins family. As we saw, Thomas undertook business ventures with his brother Elisha Baker Hopkins at least twice in his life. Thomas named one of his sons Elisha Baker Hopkins, and this Elisha became a partner in Lorenzo Dow Baker's enterprises. Thus, two men named Elisha Baker Hopkins. Thomas had a brother Richard Baker Hopkins, and he gave one of his sons that name. The Nehemiah Somes Hopkins name goes back centuries and, once again, Thomas had both a brother and a son with that name. In the Baker family there are five David Bakers in island history, as well as countless Polly Lombards! While the reuse of names sometimes confused me, I knew that such naming was intended to honor beloved relatives, and it was a convention that lasted centuries.

In his life spanning 84 years, Thomas had many roles. As a boy he had supported his fatherless family, kept his siblings together at his mother's death, and gave a home to his younger brothers when he first married. He captained many mackerel schooners, invested in a wharf, dealt in lumber, and made many property transactions; indefatigable, he became a traveling patent medicine salesman. In their later years, Thomas and Hannah Hopkins voyaged to Jamaica, in the West Indies, to visit their son Richard and their daughter Martha, who married Lorenzo Dow Baker, and their families.

Hannah and Thomas Hopkins, photographed in the late 1800s, when they resided on Baker Avenue. Photo courtesy of Joan Hopkins Coughlin

At Thomas's death in 1898, his son Richard inherited the house. Joan Hopkins Coughlin, Thomas's great-granddaughter, now uses his whalebone-knobbed walking cane, which is carved with his initials.

What became of Thomas's and Hope's children?

- Samuel, the eldest son, became a produce dealer in the Boston area.
- Martha Matilda married Lorenzo Dow Baker and lived in Jamaica, where she raised her family.
- David died in infancy.
- Thomas Jr. died at 18 in Wellfleet—with no notation of cause of death, a rare omission.
- Jerusha died at age 8 of measles.

What became of Thomas's and Hannah's children?

- Captain Elisha Baker Hopkins became L. D. Baker's partner, administering the company in Boston; later, he was an executive of the United Fruit Company.
- Richard Baker Hopkins, after years as commander of mackerel fishing vessels, moved to Jamaica to become a sugar planter.
- Nehemiah Somes Hopkins, a physician and a medical missionary for the Methodist Church, founded the first eye hospital in China. He was instrumental in erecting the memorial to the island school in 1924.
- John L. Hopkins, the youngest son, a theological student at Boston University, died of typhoid fever after visiting his Uncle Dow's family in Jamaica. His older brother's eye hospital in Beijing was named for him and was built with a substantial donation from Lorenzo Dow Baker.

The Hopkins family history illustrates the dispersion away from the Bound Brook community as seafaring life ended. Hopkins family members resettled in Wellfleet; Charlestown; Madison, New York; Jamaica, West Indies; and China.

*Captain Thomas Hopkins's cane, showing the
initials TH carved into the worn wood*

The family endured hardships and grievous losses typical of their community: Men and boys were lost at sea; mothers, young wives, sons, and daughters suffered untimely deaths from diseases that are curable today; a widow was left with many children to support; and a home was lost to fire. Nevertheless, the Hopkins family has continued on through time, and new descendants still come to Wellfleet, to the house on Baker Avenue, and to the beach at Bound Brook Island.

10

The End of Duck Harbor
and the Beginning of
Island Depopulation

IN 1850, Bound Brook Island had been near its peak of prosperity and population. Twenty-six households were home to 150 residents of all ages. But each decade more and more families left—some for Wellfleet, some for places beyond. I saw in the US Census that in 1900 the island was home to only two men: a bachelor, age 58, and a widower, age 71.

In a span of 50 years, Bound Brook had been virtually depopulated.

	NUMBER OF HOUSEHOLDS	POPULATION
1850	26	150
1860	18	84
1870	9	39
1880	9	25
1890	US Census burned; few records extant	
1900	2	2

Why did this happen?

Death of a Harbor

The island was no longer an island, and it no longer provided access for sea-going vessels. Duck Harbor, which once offered deep anchorage, slowly began silting up in the 1700s. Recall the early law forbidding livestock to feed near Bound Brook Island's beaches and the colonial lawmakers' prediction that overgrazing would cause silt to thwart navigation over time. Duck Harbor did indeed silt up, likely from that early ecological disturbance as well as from decades of sands shifting around the point in Provincetown, forming dunes on the island's western shore.

I have not been able to find the definitive date when Duck Harbor waters no longer flowed into the bay, but I think 1860 would be a good guess. No one recorded this event in the march toward depopulation. First, schooners, having a deeper draft, could not sail out to the bay; eventually, smaller boats couldn't make it out, even at high tide. Bound Brook Islanders became unable to launch their fishing boats to make their living, nor could they travel by water from Bound Brook to Wellfleet, Barnstable, Provincetown, or Boston.

Today, Duck Harbor is known as the name of a beach in Wellfleet. Today, a visitor has no sense this was once a vital outlet to the bay. The onetime basin of waters connecting to the Herring River has, over 150 years, turned into scrubby lowland overgrown with pine trees, shrubs, and, on some of its perimeter, high-bush blueberry, bountiful each July.

That's why many of Bound Brook Island's fishermen relocated with their families to the town of Wellfleet, with its spacious harbor. Or they moved to Boston and elsewhere for new opportunities. The island's school closed, and by 1880 it had been disassembled, its wood repurposed, its bell sent to Jamaica to ring atop one of the chapels there.

The start of depopulation might have been Ebenezer Atwood's move in the 1840s to the town of Wellfleet and his later move to the Boston area to deal in tea. Israel Pierce had relocated his large family and his house off the island by the early 1850s; his house appears in town on the 1858 Wellfleet map. We learned about Thomas Hopkins trying to deal lumber in Charlestown and by 1870 resettling his family homestead to Baker Avenue in the town center. After 1870, Lorenzo Dow Baker settled his family in Jamaica for most of the year, and he made his summer home, Belvernon, not on Bound Brook Island but in the center of Wellfleet.

According to the US Census for 1870, several island houses had not yet been moved; they stood unoccupied, represented by dashes on the census sheet. One particularly gruesome item I found in the Wellfleet town records in this era was of an infant discovered dead in an abandoned house. Whose child, whose house, what was this sad story?

The Wellfleet Library has large binders of photocopied sheets of details of the town's historic houses, many with photos. I was able to track many Bound Brook houses that were flaked and relocated to the town from the 1850s through the 1920s. Bound Brook Islanders resettled their homes to various streets including Cross Street, Baker Avenue, Holbrook Avenue, Ryder Court, and Chequessett Neck Road.

I noticed that the husband-and-wife householders in 1850 were mostly in their 40s and 50s. As the decades passed, those few island residents who did not move away grew older; as you see in the 1870 census below, Henry Atwood is listed as age 72 and his brother Isaiah is 68. In the 1880 census I saw that David Baker and Elisha Atwood were both 82, and Napthali Rich was 80 years old. The few houses not yet moved into Wellfleet, vacated and left behind by their owners, were rented out, likely very cheaply because times were hard, to young families who did not remain for long.

The 1870 US Census shows, on the first four lines, Bound Brook Island houses that were no longer occupied.

The Last Two Residents

A beloved Wellfleet resident, Earle Rich, describes Bound Brook Island at the turn of the century in his booklet *Cape Cod Echoes*. He relates that in the very early 1900s the two remaining Bound Brook residents lived together in what is called the Joel Atwood house. (A few years earlier, the 1900 US Census had recorded that each of these men inhabited his own dwelling.) One was Henry Atwood's nephew, Henry F. Atwood, and the other was Henry Burden, born in England. In their boyhood, Earle Rich and his brother met these two "elderly gentlemen"—Atwood, age 68, and Burden, age 81—who were relaxing and smoking pipes in front of the house.

Earle Rich told this story:

> They called to us just to ask who we were and what we were doing so far from the village. That was usually the first question we kids were asked by many of the old-timers of those days. . . . The next question was, "What are you going to do when you grow up?" We would then be reminded that Wellfleet boys always went to sea, an observation that would be followed by many recollections of their lives as boys and as men.
>
> It was during such a conversation that I learned an expression used among seafaring men: deep-sea men. I was later to learn that one of our hosts, Henry Burden, was just such a man. Our other host, Henry Atwood, was one of the men who has manned the once prosperous mackerel fleet that sailed out of Wellfleet in the mid-1800s when Duck Harbor was in full operation.

Henry Burden moved into an apartment in Wellfleet and died at age 84 in 1914. Henry F. Atwood died in town three years later.

After these two men moved to the town of Wellfleet, Bound Brook Island became uninhabited. Shortly after 1910, only six unoccupied antique houses remained. They are associated with these names: Atwood-Higgins, Elisha Atwood, Joel Atwood/Henry Atwood, Ebenezer L. Atwood, David Baker, and Byrne.

Bound Brook houses lay abandoned, wind creeping through keyholes and cracks in windows, ceilings stained and warping from leaks, gutters stuffed with leaves, shingles flown off, whole trees fallen across yards, picket fences broken. Where families ate meals and prayed together, where women cooked, baked bread, and spun wool, where girls learned needlepoint and boys whittled, where captains read the Bible by oil lamplight, where whole families slept, where babies were born: the spaces now were void. Now, silence where once children had laughed, fires crackled, and Father had closed the front door quietly before dawn as he departed for another fishing voyage.

11

———

The Herring River

AND SO BOUND BROOK ISLAND WENT FROM A THRIVING COMMUNITY of 150 inhabitants to an island where no one lived. The story of Wellfleet's Herring River, winding past the island and a part of its history, is similarly a story of loss, that of ecological disaster and the unintended consequence of a decision made with the intent to foster the town's economy.

For thousands of years the Herring River was deep and robust, until the early years of the twentieth century. I wonder what Captain Reuben Rich would think if he could see the Herring River today. I would bring him to the culvert where a stream passes under the road from town, near the turnoff onto the island. Rich, who built his schooner 200 feet from this culvert, would see a narrow stream moving very slowly. Barely navigable by a single kayak, the water is crowded with tall grasses and other vegetation.

The Herring River at the culvert, east of Bound Brook Island Road. In 2019 someone placed an armchair on a pallet there.

The River Before 1910

For millennia, the Herring River's pool of fresh water just below the Atwood-Higgins house was the precious "watering place" for the Punonakanits and, later, the colonial settlers. The abundant river herring and alewives served as food and as fertilizer in the cultivation of corn. And, yes, Captain Reuben Rich built the *Freemason* by the river and sailed it out to the bay. In the late 1800s, the town sanctioned a fishway to catch and profit from the prodigious seasonal herring run at this southeastern base of Bound Brook Island.

Glacial kettle ponds in northeastern Wellfleet are the headwaters of the Herring River, which descends on a four-mile course along valleys and around hilly landforms, finally flowing past Griffin's Island on the west and Chequessett Neck on the east into Wellfleet Harbor. Before 1910, fulsome daily tides flushed into and up the riverway.

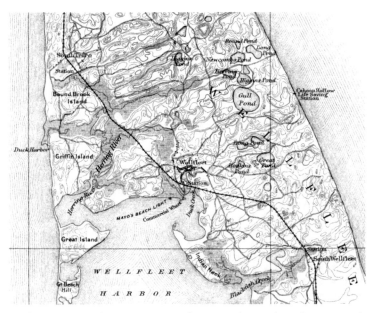

In this 1887 map, the Herring River begins in the ponds in the upper right and flows southwest, past Griffin's Island and into Wellfleet Harbor.

Countless river herring and alewives, adaptable to both saltwater and freshwater, wintered in the Atlantic Ocean. In spring they entered the "borderland" mix of fresh and salt waters at the Herring River and swam upriver to the Wellfleet ponds to lay their eggs and fertilize them with clouds of milt. The English explorer Captain John Smith described the herring run near Plymouth in 1623: "In April there is a fish most like Herring that come up into the small Brookes to spawne, and where the water is not knee deepe, they will presse up through your hands, yea though you beat at them with Cudgels, and in such abundance as incredible."

The annual herring run was a both a community social event and a lucrative source of income for the Town of Wellfleet. By 1791, the right to fish for herring was auctioned off by the town selectmen. Each Wellfleet family was permitted to take 200 fish annually, at a cost of a half-cent each. In the later 1800s, auctioning of the fishing rights brought to the town a revenue of between $409 and $667, and these proceeds paid all the elected town officials. In 1893 a sluiceway was cut between Higgins and Gull ponds, which increased the spawning grounds by 90 acres. In that year $1,035 (almost $30,000 in 2021 dollars) was bid and paid for the fishing rights.

The Fishery at Bound Brook Island

In 1896 the Wellfleet town meeting voted to move the fishery station from its then-location, likely near High Toss Road, to the foot of Bound Brook Island. The *Yarmouth Register* of February 22, 1896, reported: "Messrs. Reuben and George Williams are building a new herring house near Bound Brook Island Bridge." This move was probably prompted by two synergistic factors: First, the catch had become larger since 1893 due to the larger spawning grounds. Second, the new location offered better accessibility to markets. The Old Colony Railway, whose track was laid near Bound Brook Island in 1873, could load barrels of herring for rail transport to Boston and onward to the West Indies.

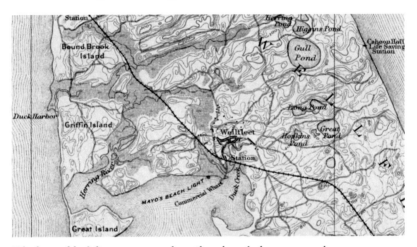

The heavy black line represents the railroad track that connected Provincetown to Boston and bordered Bound Brook Island.

A train steams across the Cape Cod landscape. THS

The Bound Brook's fishway operation included a closable channel for harvesting fish and three buildings: one for salting and barreling, a shack for storing equipment, and a storage structure beside the railroad tracks where barrels were loaded on the train's evening run to Boston. The following three photographs from 1903 show the bare landscape, which now (more than a century later) is fully greened with bushes, trees, and tall grasses.

Fishway at Bound Brook Island in 1903. The catching channel is visible in the foreground. In the nearer building, fish were salted and packed into barrels. The railroad track ran alongside the building in the background. WHSM

Another 1903 view of the fishway shows a building in the left foreground that was used for storing equipment. This smallest building still stood in the 1920s. WHSM

This 1903 view of the Herring River from Bound Brook Island, near the Atwood-Higgins House, looks southward toward Merrick's Island and the road leading to the town of Wellfleet. Parts of the fishway gates, screens, and false channel are visible. WHSM

David Belding, whose early career was supported by L. D. Baker, later became the Commonwealth of Massachusetts expert on fisheries. In his book *A Report upon the Alewife Fisheries of Massachusetts*, he described how fishways worked: During catching season (between April 1 and June 1), the migratory fish had free passage three days a week to the ponds for spawning. On the remaining four days, the stream was gated and screened off—water could pass through, but fish could not. A false channel, formed in the shape of a horseshoe and gated and screened at its upper and lower ends, was opened on these four days per week. The fish that swam into this false channel were contained and harvested.

Almost all of the "industrial" bounty caught in the late 1800s and early 1900s was salted and packed in barrels for sale off-Cape. According to David Belding, in the last decade of the nineteenth century, Wellfleet's Herring River run was the second most productive in the state. While figures are available for the income to the town for auctioning the fishing rights, I've found no figures for the income from the sale of herring by the owners of those rights. The income must have been substantial and profitable, however, to be worth the price of the fishing rights.

Fishermen gather the catch in a seine net. WHSM

Diking the River

Human intervention in the twentieth century profoundly changed the Herring River and its estuary. The precipitating factor was the mosquito. This insect was hindering Wellfleet's tourism industry, which was the town's new hope for developing the economy in the face of the continuing decline of the mackerel catch. The town and its businessmen, including the prominent Lorenzo Dow Baker, argued that the insects plagued summer visitors, who arrived in summer by train and boat to enjoy the Chequesset Inn and the growing number of little cottages for rent near Wellfleet Harbor. They believed the Herring River estuary was the breeding ground for mosquitoes. By 1905, mosquitoes had been identified as the vector for yellow fever and malaria, and fear of disease may also have motivated the citizens of Wellfleet to act.

No research seems to have been conducted to explain the cause of the abundance of mosquitoes. Did the estuary breed the prolific mosquitoes, or were several summers of heavy rain in Wellfleet to blame? The town fathers believed they could control the mosquito population by reducing the watery surface area of the Herring River estuary. Work began in 1908. Wellfleet town records state, "All work was completed on May 24, 1910, the total cost, including supervision and incidental expenses, being $20,548.86." In 2021 terms, that's $582,000.

The dike was located at the river's mouth, under the road bridge connecting Chequessett Neck and lower Griffin's Island. Before the construction of the dike, large, oxygen-rich tides had twice daily flushed the broad estuary, promoting a nurturing environment for its vegetation, marine life, insects, birds, and mammals. After construction of the dike, the tidal rhythm, which had been a daily, vigorous, two-beat heart, virtually disappeared.

Over decades, the dike reduced 1,100 acres of salt marsh grasses to 10 acres. The diminished estuary no longer provided a healthy wetland habitat for wildlife. The marsh grasses and other native plants could not thrive in the stagnant, acidic waters, and opportunistic nonnative plants clogged the waterway. Ultimately, diking created conditions that triggered the release of toxins from the soil to such an extent that vast numbers of fish were killed by the sulfurous

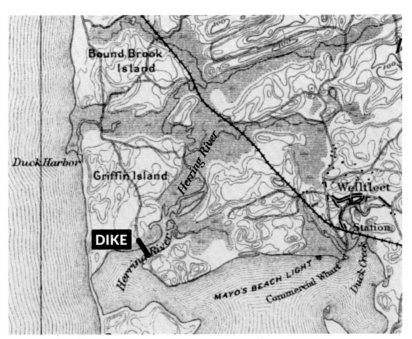

The 1910 dike crosses the mouth of the Herring River.

water. The spring herring run all but collapsed. In places, the river water today is as acidic as lemon juice.*

Diking did create "reclaimed" acreage, enough for five of nine fairways for a golf course built in 1929 and additional land for homes. However, diking by no means ended the mosquito problem for the town of Wellfleet. The town spent funds on mosquito control for decades to come—oiling the marshes, channelizing the river, and digging grid ditches to drain freshwater.

The train discontinued stops at Bound Brook Island when the herring catch declined precipitously due to the diking of the river. The town's revenue from the sale of fishing rights plummeted from highs of over $1,300 in the early 1900s to $21 in 1911.

Restoration

The local environmental organization Friends of Herring River provides a history of a campaign, undertaken in 2004, to create a restoration plan for the river and estuary. Plans call for a dike redesign that would, over years, gradually increase the tidewater flow into the Herring River; the plan includes a great deal of ancillary construction, such as raising of roads. The project, whose Phase I budget is $47 million over five years, has federal and state support.

To this day, "restoration" remains controversial in the town of Wellfleet, in part due to the specter of rising global ocean levels. Some townspeople ask whether the estuary can be returned to its 1908 condition after more than 100 years of invasion by nonnative species of vegetation and the growth of a multitude of large trees. Diking the river had many unintended consequences. Will gradual "restoration" in the time of climate change also have unintended consequences?

Not a trace remains of Bound Brook's fishway and its gates, screens, and three buildings. Hundreds of thousands of fish no longer swim upstream here to their mating grounds, nor are any harvested and shipped to Boston. Gone

---

* For a more complete description of the ecological destruction of the estuary and river I refer the reader to the website friendsofherringriver.org for a history of the tide restriction by diking and its impact over the past century.

are the teams of men with their dip nets and seines. All that remains of the operation is a curve in Old County Road.

———

I cherish a view I came upon one day while traipsing near today's Herring River stream at Bound Brook. The view is secluded, not visible from the road. If you want to see it, wear long pants and socks for protection from poison ivy and ticks. Coming from the town of Wellfleet, park on the left at the culvert just before the road turns onto the island. There's a sandy spot for one car. Make your way southward, along the stream's west bank, parting the vegetation. You'll come upon a glade of white birches, their leaves fluttering in the breeze. Above you on the hill is the Atwood-Higgins House, nearly screened by full-grown trees. Continue a little farther to where the island inhabitants for centuries came for drinking water. In this very quiet place, once the edge of a beautiful, deep river, Reuben Rich built his schooner.

———

12

The Twentieth Century
and Beyond

ON THE VERGE OF THE 1920S a new kind of inhabitant began arriving on Bound Brook Island. Many of these newcomers became part-time summer residents. Most had winter homes off-Cape and used Bound Brook as a summer retreat from their settled lives elsewhere. New people from a new age were about to discover this abandoned, beautiful place and marry it to their desires. My look at this era is selective and by no means an exact history of house ownership.

The Atwood-Higgins House and George Higgins

As we learned earlier, George Kimball Higgins, a distant descendant of the original owner of the Atwood-Higgins House, acquired the house and its ample acreage in 1919. The house had been vacant for decades, and George Higgins set about making it habitable for summertime use. By 1947 he had built eight other structures on the land, including a barn, a summer house, a guesthouse for family and friends, and a replica "country store." This final building project was prompted by nostalgia for his childhood visits to a store in rural Vermont. The "store" was actually his office, which he filled with antiques, but he also furnished it with plastic fruit and vegetables on display and fake mail in the mailboxes. He surrounded the property with miles of split rail fences, some of which still stand today.

George Higgins and his wife Katherine transferred their property, all 192 acres, to the Cape Cod National Seashore in 1961 and continued their summer occupancy for the rest of their lives. In 1975 the Atwood-Higgins House and its surrounding 24 acres were listed in the National Register of Historic Places. The National Park Service and the Olmstead Center for Landscape Preservation supported extensive research on the structures and landscape, producing a 448-page report including photographs, maps, diagrams, and a history. George Higgins's journal is an invaluable resource, describing what Bound Brook Island was like from 1919 through the 1960s, when Higgins died.

In his journal George Higgins wrote, "An old house is a constant care." The Park Service knows this all too well. Funds to maintain the main house, let alone the Higgins's beloved twentieth-century buildings, are scant to nil. Visitors on small tours arranged by the Park Service must use their imagination to visualize what the Atwood and Higgins families saw when they lived here. Still, it is a step back in time to descend the driveway, past the now-dilapidated "country store," past the whalebone fencepost, to arrive at the north side of the old house. Inside, the fireplaces are outsized, the "Indian shutters" slip out from the walls to cover the window glass in case of attack, and the wooden cupboards and old doors are a warm honey-brown. Footsteps echo in the empty house as visitors walk through.

George Higgins's "Country Store," built in 1946, unused since the early 1960s. 2021

The Ebenezer L. Atwood House

As mentioned earlier, to my knowledge Ebenezer Atwood never lived full time in the house that bears his name, which he owned fully by 1879 but only visited. This Atwood house is the antique Cape my family now inhabits in summer, a house whose wide floorboards and every cranny we know so well. It has, like every true Cape house, a borning room.

THE BORNING ROOM
IN THE EBENEZER L. ATWOOD HOUSE

Off the large keeping room
once used for cooking,
the borning room was
nearest the hearth, snug.
The sick, the dying,
or mother and newborn
bedded there for warmth,
kept close by.
               Today it's where
we scuff off sandals,
sneakers, flip-flops, toe them
under the fat bureau stuffed
with bed linen and beach towels.
On spontaneous house tours
guests admire the wainscoting,
wide floorboards, old glass
in six-by-nine panes.
But the borning room
brings us all nose-pressed
to the window of another time:
the terrible chest cold,
the day grandma died,
the day we gave birth,
or were born.

In 1918, Ebenezer's son Arthur Atwood, the last Atwood owner of this house, had to register for the draft at age 45, and he listed his residence as Wellfleet and his occupation as farmer. At one time Arthur also owned his grandfather Henry's house and land directly across the cart path. Years ago, the Hall family turned up a shovel of Arthur's, with his name burnt into the wooden handle.

In the late 1940s and early 1950s the Clark family lived in the Ebenezer Atwood house. Several years ago, their son described to me what a magical place the island had been for him to roam as a young boy. He recalled that even in the 1950s water came up to the edge of Bound Brook Island Road opposite what is now called the Baker-Biddle property, and in winter he ice-skated there. Today, that area is a wetland overgrown with blackberry, honeysuckle, and profuse shrubbery.

In the late 1950s, painter Judith Rothschild and her husband, novelist Anton Myrer, acquired the Ebenezer L. Atwood house. Judith, who owned the property until 1993, had Jack Hall, the self-trained architect and artist who became my friend so many years later, design a painter's studio with north-facing windows that today is my husband's writing studio and our guest quarters. Jack also created a dining space and kitchen off the main Cape structure.

Arthur Jesse Atwood's shovel handle. Photo courtesy of Nathaniel Hall Taylor

Memorializing the Island School

In 1924, Dr. Nehemiah Somes Hopkins, son of Thomas and Hannah Hopkins, made one of his dreams come true: He memorialized the one-room Bound Brook Island school that he and his brothers had attended for a few years before his family moved into town around 1870, when Nehemiah was 10. As mentioned earlier, Dr. Hopkins dedicated his life to Methodist missionary work in China and founded an eye hospital in Beijing that stands to this day. But Wellfleet—and especially Bound Brook Island—were deep in his heart, and Dr. Hopkins returned when he could to visit family despite the long journey by ship.

Celebrating the opening of the John L. Hopkins Memorial Methodist Hospital, Beijing. Dr. Hopkins, fifth from the right, with the Emperor's brother, fourth from right, c. 1908. WHSM

Photo of the eye hospital in Beijing, from a missionary's album. Courtesy of GCAH of The United Methodist Church

Dr. Nehemiah Somes Hopkins examining a patient,
from a missionary's album. Courtesy of GCAH of
The United Methodist Church

Before sailing home from China to Wellfleet one summer, Dr. Hopkins commissioned a bronze plaque cast in Beijing. The plaque featured an excerpt from a poem (see page 10) by Martha Sparrow Baker, a schoolteacher and the wife of his schoolmate Walter Smith Baker. The plaque was bolted to a hewn stone and brought from Eastham to Wellfleet by four-wheeled cart. On August 25, 1924, the stone was set in the earth on the site where the school, dismantled in 1880, once stood.

Dr. Hopkins raised his family in China and remained there, working. During World War II he was interned, along with his daughter, by the Japanese. He credited their survival to Chinese friends who smuggled food to them. Dr. Hopkins died at age 93 in Los Angeles and is buried in his beloved Wellfleet.

A four-wheel cart hauled the
schoolhouse memorial stone
from Eastham in 1924. Dr.
Hopkins (left) and Walter
Smith Baker stand at the
right of the cart. WHSM

The schoolhouse monument in place. Bound Brook Island was devoid of most trees and shrubs when the stone was set on this hill in 1924. WHSM

The schoolhouse monument in the same location, now wooded with pitch pine and scrub oak. The ground is blanketed in pine needles. 2021

You can easily walk to the schoolhouse memorial in the woods. The trail is accessed by a turn south off Bound Brook Island Road, at just the point that the other island road, Bound Brook Island Way, veers off to the northwest. The narrow path uphill is covered with reddish-brown pine needles. Just before you arrive at the stone, you will notice a shallow trough underfoot. That is where the old main road ran—past the front of the school— before George Higgins had the town reroute the road northward in 1945. The old town road, unused for over 75 years, has almost disappeared beneath the overgrowth of grasses, bushes, and trees. If you wondered why the memorial was placed so far from the road, you'll now understand that it was in fact placed alongside the former town road, where all passersby could see it.

Recall that the 1844 schoolhouse replaced an earlier school. Wellfleet's Earle Rich, in a 1972 article in *The Register*, wrote of having in his possession a tax bill for construction of the island school in 1818. The bill included a list of all the taxpayers, easily recognizable as island residents. This first island school was used for a Sabbath school, as mentioned in the Methodist Church records.

The Baker Homestead Becomes the Baker-Biddle Property

Ownership of the Baker House since 1935 completes the story that began with Captain David Baker in the 1790s. In 1935 the Estate of Lorenzo Dow Baker sold the homestead, which had been unoccupied for many years, to Katherine Dos Passos, wife of writer John Dos Passos—but the couple never lived there. Two years later, Katherine sold the property to Manhattan-born Princeton University graduate John "Jack" Hughes Hall, then 24, who opted for an unconventional life in the place he had fallen in love with.

When young Jack Hall acquired the Baker property, it included the Cape house and a little try house that had originally stored equipment for boiling down whale blubber on the nearby beach. Over the years Jack added structures to the property. He moved a saltbox barn from a nearby hill to use as a stable for his animals—a horse, a cow, and then sheep. Beside it he placed a barn from Pamet Point Road. That barn became his painting studio. Jack lived and farmed with his family for 12 years before he sold the house in 1949 to Francis Biddle, attorney general in Franklin Delano Roosevelt's cabinet and judge at the Nuremberg trials. Judge Biddle renovated one of the barns, and he and his wife, poet Katherine Chapin Biddle, kept individual rooms as studies, each with its own door to the outside.

The Biddles, thanks to their governmental and literary circles, hosted a stream of visitors during summers of the 1950s and '60s. Guests enjoyed cocktails on the lawn, coffee in front of the try house (with the sign "Delight" mounted under the roofline*), and meals in the blue-painted dining room.

---

* The sign was originally part of a wooden trim that wrapped around the porch of a tourist house in Provincetown. Jack Hall installed the sign over the kitchen door of the Baker House when he owned it in the 1930s.

Morning coffee, c. 1951, in front of the try house, next to the Baker homestead. Pictured (l–r): Manhattan Project scientist Howard Greyber; Fran Disner Biddle; Bob Keller, with his back to the camera; Randy Biddle; Francis Biddle. The photographer was probably Katherine Biddle. Photo courtesy of the Biddle Family Collection

Several generations of the Biddle family enjoyed the 10-acre property, mostly in the summer seasons, until it sold in 2011 and ultimately transferred via a land trust to the Cape Cod National Seashore. It is now referred to as the Baker-Biddle property. The Park commissioned an archaeological study of its newest acquisition.

ARCHAEOLOGICAL DIG INTO MYSTERY AT WELLFLEET PROPERTY
Headline in the Cape Cod Times, *September 14, 2012*

Archaeologists drill
hundreds of sample bores
at the Baker-Biddle property,
choose one to dig
painstakingly,
unearthing arrowheads,

tools of stone, a shellfish
midden, coins and shards
of lavender pottery.

For thousands of years
Punonakanits lived
here: hill-sheltered,
near a spring for drinking,
near salt water full
of fish and shellfish.
They died of disease
and the devastated
survivors left.
Captain David Baker built
his home exactly here
in the 1790s.

Deep in the dark
right under us:
the whole story.
Sandy soil,
layer after layer,
grain upon grain,
archives,
our human life.

Walking the land recently, I see that the National Park has reshingled the studio where Francis and Katherine Biddle worked. The main house is unoccupied, but perhaps it will be used by Park employees at some point. The little try house, moved hundreds of years ago from the beach, is still there, but the sign "Delight" is gone.

The meadow where Jack Hall pastured his horse is entirely overgrown. The road that once went south to north, the original driveway of the house, is so overgrown with trees, vines, and poison ivy that it is barely walkable.

Katherine Biddle's garden is a ghost of what it once was, the butterfly bush with its purple blooms gone wild, the one-time flowerbeds now shadows, the two catalpas spread huge. I see a few lilies beneath a window, stalks of brume bright yellow against an old fence. I search for arrowheads behind the two studios, where Stephen Biddle found many when he was as a child visiting his grandparents. I find none—just fallen trees, piles of brick, and a brick patio, grassy and mossed to oblivion.

More Houses for Jack Hall

Around 1950, in collaboration with the architect Warren Nardin, Jack Hall designed for himself a contemporary one-story house with a butterfly roof, mimicking the slightly raised wings of a butterfly. Jack sited it over the hill and west of the Baker property. Taking a cue from the original Bound Brook housebuilders, he nestled it within the landscape for weather protection; he did not build it high to gain a view of Cape Cod Bay. Jack lived in the house for several years before he decamped to Manhattan for almost a decade to work as an industrial designer.

In 1953 Jack Hall purchased a much-vandalized antique house that had been identified as Henry Atwood's from 1830 onward on deeds and maps. According to the Historic American Building Survey, the house is officially named the Joel Atwood House. I believe it is named in honor of the carpenter who worked on it and perhaps occupied it for a few years before inheriting the nearby house of his father, Stephen Atwood. The Joel Atwood house is the

The 1950 Hall House features perhaps the first butterfly roof on Cape Cod. Photo courtesy of Peter McMahon. 2007

house where the two old men in the century's first decade greeted the young Earle Rich and his friend from Wellfleet town. It was unoccupied in the early years of the twentieth century, and its mantel and other fine woodworked details were stolen. It's the house across the cart path from mine, the one where Jack was living when I met him for the first time on his clamshell driveway.

The house needed an enormous amount of reconstruction, which Jack undertook, aided by his strong sense of history and design. He kept the house's south face as it was and renovated only the interior and the north side, which faced a hollow and a steep uphill. He built a low-slung, one-storey painting studio near the cart road, south of the house.

In 1960–1961, Hall designed a contemporary house for *Nation* magazine editor Robert Hatch and his wife Ruth. It was sited north of his butterfly-roofed modern house. Jack Hall is justly celebrated for his design of the Hatch house, an icon of the Cape Cod Modern style. Below, one view shows the house's

Hatch House, looking north, c. 1960

Hatch House, looking west, c. 2015

graceful design, open to bay breezes, and the other shows its relationship to the bay, of which it has a stunning western prospect. This house reverted to the Cape Cod National Seashore, which allowed the Cape Cod Modern House Trust to restore it completely in 2009 after years of weather had damaged much of the wood.

THE HATCH HOUSE THAT JACK HALL BUILT

The fox heard hammering and voices,
eyed the weather-beaten structure.

All summer and fall the carpenters
enjoyed being of interest to the fox.

Each day he came, keeping distance,
as the house was repaired, restored.

Now the new wood decking is as it was,
striped with space to let sand fall through.

Thin ropes lift the outer walls
and the Bay air breezes in.

Atop a dune it sits like a box kite—
Jack's dream, made right again and true.

I discovered through property transaction records that the land Robert Hatch had bought for his house was once owned by the Hopkins family. Indeed, the cellar hole of the Hopkins house, moved to town in 1870, is less than 50 yards northwest of where Jack Hall sited the Hatch house.

By 1970, Jack and his wife Mardi had moved back from Manhattan to Bound Brook Island to live full time in the antique house he'd restored. I met him in the fall of 1993, when he was 79. Jack and Mardi Hall were the nexus of many writers, artists, and intellectuals who summered or vacationed on the Outer Cape and made their way to Bound Brook Island for cocktail parties and dinners. Mardi, originally from Philadelphia, always dressed up for these social affairs. She wore makeup, including a darkened beauty mark, sparkling silver bracelets and necklace, and Bohemian-style outfits, flowing and dark.

Time passes, as did Jack, then Mardi, and then, too soon, Jack's daughter Noa. The Joel Atwood house now adapts to the needs of children and grandchildren. And the house always needs to be cared for, its native plantings nurtured.

Jack Hall's grandson Caleb Williams restoring wooden wainscoting in the parlor of the Joel Atwood House, 2018

Elena Levin

Early in our years on the island my family developed a friendship with an-other Bound Brook neighbor, Elena Levin, who had been recently widowed. In 1962, Elena and Harry Levin bought the antique house nearest Duck Harbor. The original house that stood on that spot, where the harbormaster Samuel Rich and his family lived, had been moved off-island, to the vicinity of Wellfleet. The house on the site today was hauled overland from South Truro sometime before 1880 by seaman Michael Byrne. Byrne's youngest son John related that his family lived in the house as it was moved on logs pulled by horses. The move took place in the winter and took weeks to complete. The story goes that the Byrnes' house arrived at its new site with a turkey roasting in the oven.

The Levins' property features a structure called an icehouse, located on the edge of the one-time harbor. It is reputed to be one of the oldest buildings on the island. Jack Hall renovated it to serve as a rentable rustic cottage.

The Byrne house, imported from Truro, now the Levin house, near what was once Duck Harbor. 2020

Elena was born in 1913 in Imperial Russia, one of six children. Her father Ivan Zarudny worked as an engineer, and her mother Lena was a dedicated teacher. The years were chaotic with the Russian Revolution and the Civil War of 1917–1920. When the family lived in western Siberia, their father, learning that his arrest was imminent, left in 1919 for Harbin in Russo-Chinese Manchuria, a haven for over 100,000 White Russian émigrés. Two years later the six children witnessed their mother being arrested; she was then imprisoned and executed. Manya, the family's devoted helper for decades, kept the children together, and they reunited with their father in Harbin in 1922. Charles R. Crane, the philanthropist and one-time US ambassador to Beijing, brought the siblings to America. All six worked their way—partly with scholarship aid—through American colleges and universities; Elena attended Radcliffe College. Elena's eldest sister, Margaret "Mulya" Zarudny Freedman, associate professor emeritus at MIT, tells the family's story in her memoir *Russia and Beyond: One Family's Journey, 1908–1935*. She began writing the memoir while staying with her sister Elena on Bound Brook Island in the summer of 1993, our first summer as neighbors.

On Bound Brook Island, Elena and her husband Harry Levin (whose specialty at Harvard University, where he was a professor, was comparative literature) drew to themselves a circle of writers and intellectuals. Vladimir Nabokov observed the Levins' teenage daughter, her behavior and interests, as he was working on his novel *Lolita*. The economist John Kenneth Galbraith and the psychologist B. F. Skinner and his family also visited the Levins at Bound Brook Island.

MUSHROOM HUNTER
in memory of Elena Levin, 1912–2006

Once Elena took us mushrooming
in the island woods, lifting pads
of pine needles with her cane.
At just the age of our boy,
she'd foraged in Russia
with her sister Mulya.

She confided
she and Harry
kept a knife in their car:
you never knew
where *boletus*
would pop up after rain.

That day we sauteed
our *boletus*, salted,
slippery with butter,
cautiously, hopefully.
But taste did not translate:
we never hunted *boletus* again.

Yesterday, in another century,
it rained and today *boletus* rise from
where we meandered
following Elena
from another world
into this one.

Today the Levin house is filled with shelf after shelf of wonderful books. The twentieth and twenty-first centuries brought a plenitude of books, art, and music into many island houses, mostly summer homes now, that were once occupied year-round by maritime and farming families who sustained themselves by their labors on sea and land.

Bushwhacking for Cellar Holes

I made the acquaintance of Michael Parlante, a longtime Wellfleet local who works his own aquaculture grant and is a collector of arrowheads and artwork; as a youngster, Michael roamed everywhere on Bound Brook Island. He could show me the cellar holes of houses that had been moved to town, cellar holes I'd been unable to locate during my solitary wanderings over the island.

One Sunday we started at the "ghost location" of the *other* Joel Atwood

house, just east of the one in the Historic Register. Carpenter Stephen Atwood, one of the original settlers, lived at this crossroad (of our road and one
that was perpendicular to it and tracing north, a road that is no more). Stephen
sold half the family homestead to his son Joel in 1825; after his father's death in
1829, Joel inherited the rest of the house and lived there until his death in 1854.
This is the site where Mike and I made our first search.

BUSHWHACKING

This man with a clam rake
knows where the cellar holes are.
As a boy he explored them
for coins, soldiers' buttons,
bottles left behind
when almost everyone
moved their houses
to the village. He turns off
the sandy road and we enter
thickets of brittle twigs,
slim branches like whips.
Thorns of blackberry
snag my jacket, vines
grab my ankles.

He is so far ahead of me now
he disappears.
He calls *It's over here—*
the cellar hole of Joel Atwood's house.
He sifts earth
through his big hands,
fingers a fragment of brick,
tosses it to me to appreciate.
He claws, unearthing half-bricks,
and a row of smooth stones.

We traipse the pathless hills
to four more holes
all found by memory.

He surprises me when he stops
in a glade I've often walked
and says *The natives camped here.*
He squats, claws the topsoil,
rich brown, telltale of years of habitation.
Far below the soil, sand.
He shows me one, then another,
of these campgrounds. They say
more than the cellar holes
I'd come out to find. I have no
desire to dig in these places
which I will not call sacred,
though they are. I only want
to walk in them, by them,
in the knowledge of them.

We tramp back to my place.
I'll see you in the spring, he says,
throwing the clam rake
into the truckbed.
I finger the fragment of brick,
place it on a windowsill.
I go to my map, marking
the cellar holes and names.
But the native places I keep
to myself, quiet
as they are in the woods.

I found it uncanny how, from memory, my companion located cellar
holes of houses that had likely belonged to Daniel Rich and Rebecca Rich—
on hilly, scrubby land, with no old roads I could discern, no landmarks. At

some point I lost my sense of direction. Where had we walked from, where were we going? The past and the present made me vertiginous on that hot afternoon, and we decided to resume our search for more cellar holes on another day.

Bound Brook Island Way: The Other Road

No antique houses—by "antique" I mean houses constructed before 1850—remain on Bound Brook Island Way, the *other* island road, which forks off the main island road. At one time, many original islanders settled with their families out this way, including Eleazer Atwood and Reuben Rich, as well as the Hopkins family. But all their houses were moved off-island. Today, every house on this road was built in the twentieth century.

Signs at the beginning of Bound Brook Island Way, pointing northwest toward twentieth-century houses

The first house on this road is a Cape-style house built by composer Gardner Jencks in 1938–1939 on land purchased from the L. D. Baker estate. It is sited magnificently on a plateau with a stunning view of the bay—and, closer, of a beautiful heath of bayberry over a hill. I was told this hill had been a long-time favorite picnicking spot of Wellfleet townspeople.

Farther along Bound Brook Island Way, past the Hatch house driveway on the left and going to the road's end, is a scattering of five houses near the Wellfleet–Truro town line. These gray-shingled houses, mostly rented out all summer, perch on the rise at the shore's edge in order to get the water view so desirable in today's rental real estate market. All these houses rest on land once owned by Captain Reuben Rich, and before that, inhabited by the Punonakanits.

Behind these houses, to the east, I have found traces of old roads that were laid out carefully in 1800 and 1801. Today, those one-time sandy roads are completely grassed over.

Twentieth-century Bound Brook Island houses near the Wellfleet–Truro boundary; all are gray-shingled, sited high, and facing west for a view of the bay.

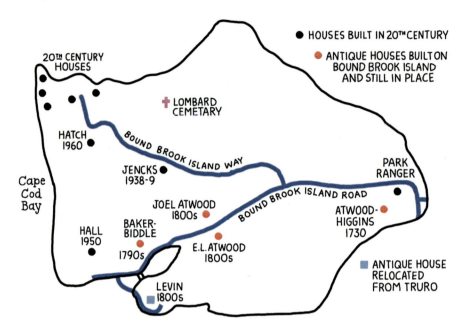

Today's Bound Brook Island, with its two roads, five antique houses, and nine houses built in the twentieth century

The location of Captain Reuben Rich's house's cellar hole remained a mystery to me for a long while. However, once I determined where the second Hopkins house had been located, near today's Hatch House, the 1848 Coast Survey map allowed me to pinpoint the Reuben Rich house site. It is in a protected low spot just beyond a curve in the narrowest part of Bound Brook Island Way, in strict alignment with the old road that went north from the Baker property.

Like all the houses built on the island in the 1700s and 1800s, Captain Rich's house nestled into the land so that it was sheltered from storms. No one in those days built their house up high or near the dunes for a water view. I saw that Captain Rich could walk out his back door, on the north side, to climb one of the highest hills of the island. From there he could survey this panorama: to the south, Nauset; to the west, Cape Cod Bay waters and the distant shoreline of the mainland; and Provincetown curving round. A beautiful world.

Epilogue

I AM NOT A HISTORIAN, geologist, or anthropologist. I am simply someone who fell in love with a place. How was this one square mile once an island but an island no more? How was this land of hills and ravines formed? Why was there virtually no vegetation in photos I saw from the early twentieth century, given that old-growth forests covered the land when the *Mayflower* arrived? Who lived here, how did they live, and why did they leave? I've spent years reading books, town records, and archives to tell the story. I have walked and looked and mused.

I came across a sentence Peter McMahon and Christine Cipriani wrote about my neighbor, the artist and self-taught architect Jack Hall, in their book *Cape Cod Modern*. They wrote, "Hall was deeply interested in the idea of Bound Brook Island as a rural paradise." Yes, that is what I apprehended when we first drove onto the island, down its sandy road, when I saw for the first time the weathered antique house through the wild hedge, the house that eventually would be in our care. The house was a dream, like an image in a miniature diorama, a kind of rustic perfection. And so too the island turned out to be, as we arrived summer after summer. The magic has not worn away, not with lawnmowing, or gypsy moths, or septic tank troubles, or repair after repair. After all, "an old house is a constant care"—we knew that from the very first. To this day, it is still a paradise, almost as much as it was in the late 1930s when a young Jack Hall arrived on the Cape and decided to settle here, farm the land, paint his canvases, and raise a family.

As I've suggested a few times, this island still holds some secrets. Where on the island were those three ecstatic camp meetings held in the full moon of August in 1823, 1824, and 1825? Who was the last seafarer to navigate his boat out to the bay from Duck Harbor before it was sealed with silt and sand dunes? What brought the young Black couple, Charles and Sarah Pope, to the island in 1850?

Is Bound Brook Island a microcosm of our country, our world? The Wampanoag's thriving population was diminished by diseases introduced by explorers and traders before the *Mayflower* arrived. Those who survived were driven from their long-inhabited lands, as were indigenous populations across the continent. The environmental degradation visited upon Bound Brook Island—the thoughtless, extreme extraction from the land by forest cutting, by relentless grazing of herds of sheep and cattle, by horses—echoes in today's polluted rivers, air, and earth.

The depopulation of Bound Brook Island can't be compared to the flight of environmental refugees we see all over the world. Unlike those millions of refugees, most of whom are unwanted anywhere, the families who left Bound Brook Island established themselves in the town of Wellfleet and beyond with relative ease.

Bound Brook Island escaped the twentieth-century building boom that characterized most of Cape Cod. Large tracts were held by the L. D. Baker Estate, George Higgins, and Jack Hall, all of whom wanted to preserve the land and rarely sold off any portion of it. When the Cape Cod National Seashore (CCNS) was established in 1961, all of Bound Brook Island was contained within it. The CCNS prohibited new home building, and thus the island was preserved as it was: with five antique houses, one antique try house, one antique icehouse, and fewer than 20 twentieth-century buildings, including nine houses (the Park ranger's, Jencks House, Hatch House, Hall's butterfly house, and five rental properties in the northwest), several studios, and George Higgins's rustic structures.

At the end of every summer I brought the island back with me to western Massachusetts.

THE WALK I TAKE
TO FALL ASLEEP AT NIGHT

In bed, eyes closing,
I stand at the screen door
with its gingerbread frame,
look past the brick path,
edged in acid green moss,
across broad lawn. I pass
the English oak, branches
spreading deep shade,
the Adirondack chairs, white
speckled with tiny acorns.
I'm heading to the slender cut
in the wild hedge, turning left
onto the old cart road,
sand warm on bare feet
after the cool grass.

            The road
shadowed by locusts and pine
breaks into full light as I round
contours of the old estuary.
Listen: cricket chorus and
cicada's long high midsummer
song. A breeze stirs the grasses,
ragweed, Queen Anne's lace,
thorny rose, nightshade's tiny
purple blooms, and finally

honeysuckle, its nectar
sweetening the air . . .
                           all waft
me on my way,
toward the dunes,
the beach, which,
falling asleep,
I never reach.

Today, Bound Brook Island is spacious in its one square mile, and it is very green since trees and shrubs reclaimed their place on the land. Cape Cod writer Robert Finch once spoke of the island's "quiet abandonment"— a poignant phrase that captures the essence of its history, its serenity. One might also say "its hush" if not for the cicadas, the songbirds, an occasional car, and sometimes the susurrus of waves on its still-nameless bay beach.

For me, the spirits of Bound Brook Island linger in its air: Jack and Mardi Hall, Noa Hall, Reuben Rich, Susannah Hopkins, Sarah Pope, Elena Levin, and many more. But the older spirits, who took good care of the land, still speak to me, and to us, over time.

THE OLD ONE

For hundreds of years he has lived here
near the brook he calls Sapokonisk.
Once he fished herring with a weir,
hunted deer in the tall woods.
His woman grew corn on the hillside.
He watched the New Ones fell trees,
build homes and make fire inside.
He saw the slaughter of blackfish,
fat boiled in big pots on the beach.
He saw flocks of sheep, herds of cattle
eating every tip of green, then winds
blowing away the soil. He saw a cross

twirling on the hill, and along the creek,
vats drying seawater, leaving white crystals.

He has seen it all: how his people
died of disease, how the harbor
silted up, how the river grew dank
no longer cleansed by the tides.
He saw gleaming rail laid, and a huge beast
smoking, roaring over the land.
Then the beast left, and grasses
covered its path.

        He keeps walking
the old trails, up and over
large crenellations of the ice age,
over heather and bearberry,
mosses of every green,
staying behind the oaks grown
tall again. In the old places
he digs arrowheads,
and rubs them.
Atop a stone once,
he left one for me.

The breach in the dunes at Duck Harbor Beach, 2021. Photo courtesy of John Portnoy

Note: Overwash at
Duck Harbor Beach, 2020–2021

IN NOVEMBER 2020, the high tides of the full moon breached a low dune at Duck Harbor Beach on Bound Brook Island. Waves of seawater from Cape Cod Bay washed into the shrubby evergreen lowlands that were once Duck Harbor and the estuary of the island. This had not occurred for more than 150 years, by my reckoning. It had been that long since the island's only harbor had silted and duned up, blocking resident mariners from the bay and their fishing livelihood and prompting them to move off-island. Slowly, over years, the sea-level land had greened with highbush blueberry shrubs, raspberry and blackberry canes, pine and locust trees, honeysuckle, Queen Anne's lace, and a myriad of other plants, including swaths of poison ivy.

In early March 2021, a YouTube video documented the bay waves washing in again. In June I walked southward down the beach to the breach, and I saw the dune sands spread inland like a vast tablecloth. I saw the graying of shrubs, and the tall pines, usually vibrant green, had turned rusty brown, dying from the invasion of saltwater.

Trees and shrubs dying from inundation by saltwater; beach sand splayed inland; view eastward on Duck Harbor Beach in June 2021

It's now the end of July 2021. At the full moon last week, 12-foot tides again washed over into the estuary basin, and I saw deeper puddles in the growth alongside Bound Brook Island Road; the stagnant pools of previous overwashes were "refreshed" by this month's tides.

Seawater invaded these lowlands this summer, pooled, and became brackish, creating a hospitable breeding ground for small saltwater mosquitoes. The infestation extended far beyond the island. These mosquitoes, we're told, can fly 10 or so miles from their birthplace—to most of Wellfleet and much of Truro. Another larger and more aggressive species of mosquito would hatch in late August.

The entire overwash area lies within the Cape Cod National Seashore. The National Park Service must abide by NPS Management Policies set in 2006 about larvicide and pesticide applications. In early July 2021, in an attempt to control the mosquito population on its nonprivate land holdings on

Bound Brook Island, the Park obtained a limited-time permit to hire an organization to apply larvicide. Unfortunately, many of the stagnant pools targeted for treatment were inaccessible due to dense overgrowth.

In the absence of effective control of these mosquito breeding grounds and the resulting "plague" of mosquitoes, residents on private land in the Park and residents of greater Wellfleet and Truro took matters into their own hands: They contracted for regular pesticide applications on their property. The active ingredients in several such applications are broad-spectrum chemicals that kill insects indiscriminately; an active ingredient in one pesticide is lethal to aquatic invertebrates. Most owners had pesticide applied to their property every other week; others purchased pesticide sprays and applied them themselves.

Without pesticide application, getting to one's car from the house was like running a gauntlet. The biting saltwater mosquitoes gathered like a mist around one's head and all over one's body, and not just at dusk, but all day long. All summer, weeding my garden was nigh impossible, and most everyone gave up cooking, eating, reading, and playing outdoors on their property.

My understanding is that the Park Service could not more aggressively deal with the mosquito infestation because these mosquitoes were a "nuisance," not a public health emergency. A public health emergency would be declared if, for example, these mosquitoes carried the West Nile virus or the Eastern equine encephalitis (EEE) virus, lethal to humans. What seems left outside consideration are the long-term effects on all forms of life of the pesticides applied biweekly all over Wellfleet and Truro by property owners this year and in years to come.

The *Provincetown Independent* reported a Park staffer saying that the Herring River Restoration Project—slowing opening a new dike at Chequessett Neck and eventually restoring the large Herring River estuary—will "solve the mosquito problem in the long term." This is open to debate, in my view. What is the meaning of "long term"? In 3 years, or 20, 40, or 100 will the Herring River Restoration Project "solve the mosquito problem"?

The main idea is that the restored tidal flushing in and out of the Herring River estuary would do away with stagnant breeding pools on Bound Brook Island. Construction of a new dike with movable panels to gradually allow more tidal flow is slated to be finished in 2023. There are many proposals for the managed opening; the current recommendation is for the first opening to be set at 0.2 inch of additional tide, increased to 20 inches by the end of the first year and to remain at that level for the second and third years, 2024 and 2025. The measured, careful opening makes a great deal of sense—in contrast with the sudden, almost-complete narrowing of the Herring River in 1910.

I wonder, though: Is this tidal increase of the Herring River estuary going to have any effect on Bound Brook Island's Duck Harbor estuary?

Duck Harbor filled with sediment and sand beginning in the 1600s and continuing through the mid-1800s. Its one-time outlet to the bay was closed with a small dike installed in 1909, and there are no plans to open it. Since 1909, what was once the harbor has filled densely with trees, bushes, and all matter of vegetation—and a century of decomposed organic material. Again, the question is: When will there be daily tidal movement of water in the Duck Harbor estuary? It is only *moving* water that stops mosquitoes from breeding. Do we know that the area that was once Duck Harbor can receive tidal ebb and flow? Or is it too filled with sediment and vegetation to allow that to occur? If it cannot be affected by tidal flow, then the stagnant mosquito-breeding pools are likely to continue to be an issue not only for the next few years but for decades to come.

Perhaps we need a plan for mosquito control that does not rely on the faint possibility of the Herring River Restoration solving the problem.

No one expected seawater to enter Duck Harbor ever again—but it has. This situation presents the twenty-first century island residents, National Park Service, and residents of Wellfleet with new challenges: to develop a plan to control the mosquito population and to face the next transformation of Bound Brook Island.

July 2021, Bound Brook Island

List of Maps

Glossary

aeolian A descriptive term for processes that pertain to wind activity, specifically the wind's ability to shape a surface. The word is derived from the name of the Greek god Aeolus, keeper of the winds.

blackfish A small whale, sometimes called a grampus whale or pilot whale. Oil derived from its blubber was used to fuel lamps and lubricate delicate mechanisms.

Bound Brook The shortened name for Bound Brook Island; the island designation is often left off as superfluous, as in "I live on Bound Brook."

camp meetings Religious gatherings in forested settings, promoted mostly by Methodists, that originated in the early 1800s in Kentucky. The first Cape Cod camp meeting (or revival) was held in South Wellfleet in 1819. For three years—from 1823–1825—Bound Brook Island was the site for camp meetings, with travelers arriving by wagon, horse, and packet boat. The gatherings, held in August and lasting from four to six days, featured tents, plank seating, and a preaching stand. The camp meetings were reported on by *Zion's Herald*, the Methodist weekly newspaper in Boston.

Cape (house) The Cape Cod dwelling of the early 1700s through mid-1800s on Bound Brook Island was adapted from simple house structures in England. They were built in three sizes. (See drawing.) A half-Cape could be expanded to a three-quarter or full Cape. On the main floor, a half-Cape had approximately 500 square feet, a three-quarter Cape, 800 square feet, and a full Cape, 1,000 square feet. All three were similar in layout. Inside the south-facing door, a staircase led to the small upper level, which was often where children slept; a south parlor let in most of the day's sunlight. The north-facing door opened to the keeping room with its large open hearth for daily living (including cooking, dining, and gathering). Houses were sited with a strict north–south orientation. The south-facing exterior was always sided in clapboards, and the rest of the house was sided in shingles that weathered to "Cape Cod gray."

Cape Cod National Seashore (CCNS) A national park encompassing 43,607 acres on Cape Cod. Created in August 1961 by President John F. Kennedy, it includes nearly 40 miles along the Atlantic eastern shore of Cape Cod, in Provincetown, Truro, Wellfleet, Eastham, and Orleans. It is one of 10 national seashores administered by the US National Park Service.

delta A low-lying, flat surface at the mouth of a river, usually triangular.

drift The general term for all glacial deposits, both those laid down by ice and those transported by meltwater.

flake (As in "The house was *flaked* and moved to Wellfleet village.") The disassembly of a house by cuts or *flakes*, many of which were jagged, like jigsaw puzzle pieces. Wellfleet historian Earle Rich wrote that the cuts were made jagged so that when the house was put back together, a piece would fit only one way and would be stronger.

foreset bed A steeply dipping bed of sediment deposited at the front of a delta.

jig (for mackerel) Invented about 1820, a line with a hook; its shank had a plummet of lead or pewter as a weight. A mass of chopped bait was cast overboard to attract mackerel to the surface while the vessel drifted. Crew members stood on deck, leaning over the ship's sides, and each let out two or three jigs hooked with slivers of bait. The crew flipped mackerel into barrels. Hand-jigging was more efficient than trailing bait behind the vessel, and lucrative mackerel fishing yields encouraged captains to shift from day fishing to longer trips, often lasting months. Jigging could easily be done by boys, so some as young as 10 were taken on fishing journeys.

kames Mounds, unsorted gravel, and sand deposited by a melting ice sheet. We experience them as steep hills.

kettles Small or large pond-size impressions in the landscape caused by the weight of massive chunks of ice broken off the Laurentide glacier as it receded northward. On the Cape, some depressions fed by springs became "kettle ponds"; others, without water, are smooth depressions with steep sides.

lights Small panes of glass positioned in a horizontal panel above exterior doors. Cape houses built on Bound Brook Island before 1900 traditionally had five lights above north-facing and south-facing doors.

Lower Cape The "elbow" of the Cape, including Harwich, Chatham, Brewster, and Orleans.

mackerel (Atlantic) Slender, fast-swimming fish, 12–18 inches in length, weighing 1–3 lb. They winter in deeper offshore waters but move closer to shore in spring and summer. The fishing season for Atlantic mackerel was May–November.

memory map An informal, hand-drawn map of an area, showing features recollected by a one-time inhabitant. It may include houses with names of owners, roads, rivers, and other details. Dr. Nehemiah Somes Hopkins drew one such map of Bound Brook Island, recollecting it as it was around 1860, the year in which he was born there.

Mid-Cape The "bicep" of the Cape's arm, including Yarmouth, Dennis, and Barnstable/Hyannis.

Nauset A small tribe of people, perhaps numbering 500 around 1621, who lived in what is present-day Cape Cod, Massachusetts, east of the Bass River on land occupied by their closely related neighbors, the Wampanoags. Although a distinct tribe, they were often subject to the Wampanoags' overlordship and shared many aspects of culture and agricultural practices with them.

nine-over-six An arrangement of panes of glass to form a window. In colonial days, window glass was precious and expensive. Cape Codders arranged small panes in groups to form their windows. A common arrangement was nine panes (3 x 3) over six (3 x 2).

Outer Cape The "forearm" of the Cape, including Eastham, Wellfleet, Truro, and Provincetown.

packet In the 1700s and 1800s, a small boat, initially powered by wind and later by steam, that hauled freight and goods—the cargo was often loaded as individual "packets." Later, packet boats carried passengers. Depending on its size, a packet in the era before 1840 could carry 25–50 passengers. Travel by packet from Boston to the Cape was preferred over coach travel in the early 1800s. From Boston, a packet boat usually took four or five hours to reach Wellfleet; the voyage to Barnstable, farther south, took about eight hours. Travel by stagecoach from Boston to Wellfleet could take two days.

Pleistocene The geological epoch that lasted from about 1.6 million years ago to 10,000 years ago, spanning the world's recent period of repeated glaciations. Often called the Ice Age.

Punonakanit people Members of the Wampanoag Federation and part of the Nauset tribe who lived on the Lower Cape. Punonakanits lived in the area that is today Wellfleet. Their land itself was called Punonakanit. According to Durand Echevarria in *A History of Billingsgate*, the Punonakanit lived alongside the English settlers, but disease claimed all but 11 of them by 1694; by 1770, no Punonakanit was living in Wellfleet.

river herring Either of two species of fish that have been longtime swimmers and breeders in Atlantic coast waters and streams: alewives and blueback herring. They swim in large schools in the waters off the Continental Shelf between Nova Scotia and Cape Hatteras. In their spring spawning migration, the fish leave their huge schools and disperse as they return to their river of birth. An individual fish may spawn five or six times over that many years. Because they migrate from the saline sea up into fresh water to spawn, they are termed an anadromous species.

saltworks Operations to produce salt from evaporated seawater using solar power, a series of large vats, and windmills for pumping water to the vats.

Cape Codders needed salt primarily to preserve catches of mackerel and other fish.

Sapokonisk The Punonakanit name for the brook the English colonists named Bound Brook. It means "watery outlet" or "miry field," as in marshland.

schooner A type of sailing ship defined by its rig configuration. It has two or more masts, the foremast slightly shorter than the mainmast. Its sails are set along the line of the keel—along the spine of the ship—rather than perpendicular to the keel as in square-rigged ships such as the *Mayflower*. Schooners were developed off the coast of North American in the early 1700s for fishing and local trade. Many captains prized schooners for their speed, versatility, upwind prowess, and relatively small crews.

seine A type of fishing net. The modern seine boat, or trawler, was invented by a Gloucester fisherman in 1855. By 1865, seine fishing had replaced hand-jigging to catch mackerel. The purse seine is a drag net that can be closed at the bottom so fish cannot escape. This new method required the strength of adult men and allowed for a smaller fishing crew.

shallop An open wooden workboat, small enough to row but having one or two sails. It was about 30 feet long, with a draft of about two feet, suitable to navigate shallow waters. A shallop was quartered and fit into the *Mayflower* for the Atlantic passage in 1620. It took more than two weeks for the ship's carpenter to ready the boat for service.

try works Equipment used in the rendering of the blubber of whales into whale oil. Try works were originally set up on the beach in the open air. Eventually, whaling ships had their own try works on board, usually two or three large metal pots near the mainmast, set within brickwork and fired by wood.

Upper Cape The western "shoulder" of Cape Cod, beginning at the bridges at Bourne and Sagamore and including Sandwich and Falmouth.

ventifact A stone eroded and polished by wind-transported sand and silt.

Wampanoag A loose confederation of tribes that lived in southeastern Massachusetts and Rhode Island at the beginning of the seventeenth century, at the time of first contact with English colonists. Their territory included the islands of Martha's Vineyard and Nantucket. Their population numbered in the thousands; 3,000 Wampanoags lived on Martha's Vineyard alone.

Time Line

THE NAUSET TRIBE inhabited Cape Cod for millennia. Their name for the land now known as Wellfleet was Punonakanit.

1614 and 1617 A great pestilence, now thought to be leptospirosis, a bacterial infection transmitted by rat urine, desolated the indigenous population of the southern New England shore.

1620 The *Mayflower* arrived; the Plymouth Colony was established.

1640 Seven Plymouth colonists settled across Cape Cod Bay from Plymouth, in Orleans and Eastham (then called Nauset). In later years they and others acquired more land northward for farming and grazing livestock.

1666 English colonists purchased the area that is now Wellfleet, including Bound Brook Island, from a Punonakanit chief named Lieutenant Anthony.

1666–1795 Hardwoods were harvested for ships' masts and shipbuilding, housebuilding, fencing, and fuel. Herds of sheep, cattle, and swine denuded the hills and dales of virtually all vegetation.

1690 (approximately) Colonists who had acquired land north of a brook set a boundary stone by a white oak where the brook entered the bay. They named the waterway Bound Brook. This was the boundary between Truro and the North Precinct of Eastham, sometimes known as Billingsgate and later incorporated as Wellfleet.

1712 Truro and Eastham selectmen installed a new boundary of rocks at Bound Brook because the first boundary marker was washed away by the sea.

1723 Inhabitants of the hamlet of Billingsgate were denied incorporation as a town separate from Eastham. Incorporation as a separate town was approved 40 years later; see below.

1730 Thomas Higgins and others began to settle with their families on Bound Brook Island.

1763 Wellfleet, formerly known as Billingsgate, was established as a town by the General Court. Bound Brook Island lies in the town's northwest. The Town of Wellfleet comprises 35.4 square miles, of which 19.8 are land and 15.6 are water.

1768 A General Court law limited livestock grazing on Bound Brook beaches and shore.

1770 The native oysters had died out (according to Henry David Thoreau in his book *Cape Cod*); the cause is unknown. Thereafter, oyster stocks were brought from other regions to cultivate in Wellfleet waters.

1775–1780 British blockade. Over these years, whaling ships rotted in Wellfleet Harbor, marking the end of whaling for Wellfleet. Thereafter, cod and then mackerel fishing became the main industry for Wellfleet mariners.

1799–1800 The schooner *Freemason*, capable of "100-ton burden," was built on Bound Brook Island's eastern shore on the Herring River by early resident Captain Reuben Rich. It was the first ship built in Wellfleet.

1800–1801 Roads (cart paths) were laid out by nine Bound Brook residents and approved by the Town of Wellfleet.

1800–1810 (approximately) Dunes began to form at the mouth of Bound Brook; eventually, the brook no longer flowed into Cape Cod Bay.

1818 The first Island School was built.

1821 Sabbath school began on Bound Brook Island, held in the Island School House.

1823–1825 Methodist camp meetings, each almost a week long, convened outdoors on Bound Brook Island in August with renowned preachers Lorenzo Dow and Father Taylor. Three packet boats sailed from Boston with attendees for the 1824 meeting.

1837 Thirty saltworks had been established in Wellfleet, including two on Bound Brook Island: one on the Captain Baker property and another to the north, near Reuben Rich's. Salt was a necessity for preserving fish to sell to markets off-Cape. By the 1880s, the Cape's salt-making industry had been abandoned. Domestic salt mines were discovered in western New York, and salt could be transported easily to markets by rail.

1844 The second Island School was built at the location of the former school.

1850 Bound Brook Island was perhaps at its peak population, with 26 households and 150 persons.

1850–1860s (approximately) Bound Brook Island's only navigable harbor—Duck Harbor—gradually silted up; ultimately, it was transformed into a beach. When mariners on Bound Brook could no longer access the bay for fishing and transportation, they moved their families and houses to Wellfleet village.

1854–1855 Bound Brook Island's Black residents, a young married couple, were severely injured in a steamboat accident in Boston Harbor as they were on their way to Maine; they return to Wellfleet and eventually to the island.

1859 The Lombards of South Truro established a small family cemetery in northwest Bound Brook as the final resting place for Mary Lombard, dead of smallpox. The Truro town fathers, for health reasons, had refused to allow her burial in the town cemetery.

1873 Cape Cod Railroad extended its tracks from Wellfleet, along eastern and northern Bound Brook Island, to Truro and Provincetown. Passenger service ended in 1937; freight transport continued until the mid-1960s.

1880 The Island School, built in 1844, was torn down and its timber was re-purposed elsewhere.

1880 Mackerel fishing, for decades a lucrative industry for Wellfleet, began to decline and by 1900 had virtually ended.

1881 Lorenzo Dow Baker, born on Bound Brook Island in 1840, formed the L.D. Baker Company to cultivate and import bananas from Jamaica. The enterprise morphed into the Boston Fruit Company in 1885 and, in 1899, to the United Fruit Company.

1892 Wellfleet's herring fishery was relocated to the eastern end of Bound Brook Island, on the Herring River. From 1892 through 1909 the train stopped at the fishery to load barrels of herring for delivery to markets off-Cape.

1902 Lorenzo Dow Baker's Chequesset Inn opened in the town of Wellfleet, presaging the tourist industry.

1905 The Wellfleet Town Meeting voted to appoint a committee and petition the Legislature to build a dike across the Herring River. It was intended to control mosquitoes that affected the nascent tourist industry in the nearby town center and to create additional land.

1910 The construction of the dike across the Herring River was completed. Over the next century, the dike dramatically altered and damaged the Herring River and the estuary.

1910 The herring fishery at Bound Brook Island, comprising three buildings, stopped operations due to the diminished herring run.

1910–1919 (approximately) Bound Brook Island was uninhabited. In 1919, George Higgins, a distant relative of the original owner, acquired the Atwood-Higgins property to use as a summer home.

1924 The Island School House memorial, a boulder and plaque, was placed where the school once stood. Bound Brook native Dr. Nehemiah S. Hopkins devised the memorial.

1927 and 1945 At George Higgins's request, the Town of Wellfleet twice moved the older part of the Bound Brook Island Road northward to accommodate his project: construction of a replica Vermont-style general store and other buildings on the land north of the Atwood-Higgins house.

1937 John Hughes (Jack) Hall purchased the Captain David Baker property and began his residence on the island, inhabiting a succession of three homes over 60 years.

1950 Jack Hall, with Warren Nardin, began to build his own modern butterfly-roof house close to the beach, nestled out of sight so as not to mar the dunes-only shoreline of the bay.

1953 Jack Hall purchased and eventually began restoration of the Joel Atwood antique Cape house, which had been owned by the Henry Atwood family from approximately 1830–1929.

1960–1961 Jack Hall designed the Hatch House for *Nation* editor Robert Hatch. This house, now owned by the National Park Service and restored by the Cape Cod Modern House Trust, is considered to be the iconic Cape Modern house.

1961 The Cape Cod National Seashore (CCNS) was created, incorporating all of Bound Brook Island. Although private property was still held on the island, the Atwood-Higgins House and significant undeveloped acreage were deeded to the Park by individuals. No new house construction was allowed on the island. The Park Service extensively studied and documented the Atwood-Higgins house and made it available for public tours.

2004–2005 Planning for restoration of the Herring River began. By 2008, the Herring River Restoration Committee had been established.

2012 The Cape Cod National Seashore acquired the Baker-Biddle property and commissioned an archaeological dig that confirmed habitation on the land for thousands of years.

2020 The Duck Harbor Beach dune was breached, allowing bay waters into the one-time Duck Harbor and its estuary for the first time in over 100 years.

Documents

THE FOLLOWING PAGES 156–160 display the 1850 US Census for Bound Brook Island residents in the town of Wellfleet, Massachusetts.

Page 161 reproduces the masthead and an article from the abolitionist newspaper *The Liberator*, December 1, 1854.

Bound Brook Island residents begin on Line 17 with Samuel Rich.

SCHEDULE I.—Free Inhabitants in *Town of Wellfleet* in the County of *Barnstable* St of *Massachusetts* enumerated by me, on the *7o* day of *September* 1850. *Isaiah Diffield* Ass't Mar

		The Name of every Person whose usual place of abode on the first day of June, 1850, was in this family.	Age.	Sex.	Color, white, black, or mulatto.	Profession, Occupation, or Trade of each Male Person over 15 years of age.	Value of Real Estate owned.	Place of Birth, Naming the State, Territory, or Country.				Whether dea dumb, blind, i Idiotic, paupe convict.
1	2	3	4	5	6	7	8	9	10	11	12	13
1		James "	16	m		*Mariner*		*Mass*			1	
2		Lorenzo Cool	16	m		*Mariner*		"		1		
3		Nathaniel D O Wiley	21	m		"		"				
4	371 441	Freeman Cobb	24	m		"		"		1		
5		Adelia M "	23	f				"				
6		Amelia F "	2	f				"				
7	442	Nathaniel W Rich	25	m		"		"		1		
8		Catherine "	24	f				"				
9		Ellen G "	3	f				"				
10	372 443	Henry Atkins	60	m	1	"		"				
11		Thankful	36	f				"				
12		John Bennis	17	m	1	"		"		1		
13		Caroline Rich	13	f				"		1		
14		Henry F "	7	m				"		1		
15		Robert L "	5	m				"				
16	444	Sabra Atwood	76	f			100	"				
17	373 445	Samuel Rich	53	m		*Farmer*	600	"		1		
18		Polly L "	46	f				"				
19		Samuel R "	21	m		*Mariner*		"		1		
20		Newel B "	19	m		*Sail maker*		"		1		
21		Obediah "	16	m		*Mariner*		"		1		
22		Snow "	15	m				"		1		
23		Sally B "	13	f				"		1		
24		Albin B "	9	m				"		1		
25		Melissa H "	8	f			1	"		1		
26		Isaac S "	6	m				"		1		
27		Lucy L "	2	f				"				
28	374 446	David Baker	52	m	1	"	900	"				
29		Betsy N "	52	f				"				
30		Reuben H "	25	m	1	"		"				
31		David "	23	m		"		"				
32		Thankful R "	20	f				"				
33		Deborah B Smith	22	f				"				
34		Edwin L Baker	15	m				"		1		
35		Ruth "	12	f				"		1		
36		Lorenzo D "	10	m				"				
37		Walter S "	4/12	m				"				
38		John Kitchery	25	m		"		N.S.				
39		Nancy "	21	f				"				
40		Rachel "	9	f				"				
41	375 447	Edward Hopkins	31	m	1	"	500	*Mass*				
42		Sally	30	f				"				

1 m 24

177

89

	Families numbered in the order of visitation.	The Name of every Person whose usual place of abode on the first day of June, 1850, was in this family.	Age.	Sex.	Color.	Profession, Occupation, or Trade of each Male Person over 15 years of age.	Value of Real Estate owned.	PLACE OF BIRTH. Naming the State, Territory, or Country.	Married within the year.	Attended School within the year.	Persons over 20 y'rs of age who cannot read & write.	Whether deaf and dumb, blind, insane, idiotic, pauper, or convict.	
1	2	3	4	5	6	7	8	9	10	11	12	13	
		Isaiah S Hopkins	6	m				Mass		1			1
		Unknown "	1/2	m				"					2
76	448	Edward do	57	m		Farmer		"					3
		Joanna "	56	f				"					4
		Benj "	19	m		Mariner		"					5
		Joanna "	23	f				"					6
		Ephriam G Knowles	24	m		"		"					7
77	449	Reney Atwood	57	m		Farmer		"					8
		Polly "	50	f				"					9
		Medford C "	24	m		Mariner		"					10
		Elisha R. "	11	m				"		1			11
		Mary L "	14	f				"		1			12
78	450	Isaiah Atwood	45	m		Farmer	400	"					13
		Martha "	40	f				"					14
		Henry F "	8	m				"		1			15
		Isaiah "	5	m				"					16
		Freeman N "	3	m				"					17
79	451	Samuel Baxter	57	m		"	500	"					18
		Sarah "	51	f				"					19
		Chas "	14	m				"		1			20
		Angeline "	12	f				"		1			21
80	452	Hames Atwood	44	m		Mariner	400	"					22
		Elisa J "	21	f				"					23
		Elisa C "	6	f				"		1			24
		Elijah N "	4/12	m				"					25
		Hames "	17	m		"		"					26
		Ruth C "	18	f				"					27
	453	Ruth Rich	64	f			50	"					28
		Ruth Atwood	66	f				"					29
		Joel "	41	m		"		"					30
81	454	Abram Atwood	42	m		"	500	"					31
		Elisabeth "	36	f				"					32
		Emily G "	18	f				"					33
		Elisabeth N "	16	f				"		1			34
		Clarissa "	15	f				"		1			35
		Abram "	13	m				"		1			36
		James H "	7	m				"		1			37
82	455	Mercy Rich	53	f			300	"					38
		Elisha P "	24	m				"					39
		Seth "	27	m		Pedlar		"					40
83	456	Levi O Atwood	51	m		Mariner	550	"					41
		Nancy "	48	f				"					
			m 24										

SCHEDULE I.—Free Inhabitants in *Town of Wellfleet* in the County of *Barnstable* S
of *Massachusetts* enumerated by me, on the *7* day of *September* 1850. *Lincoln Siffoal* Ass't Mar

	Dwelling-houses numbered in the order of visitation	Families numbered in the order of visitation	The Name of every Person whose usual place of abode on the first day of June, 1850, was in this family.	Age	Sex	Color	Profession, Occupation, or Trade of each Male Person over 15 years of age.	Value of Real Estate owned	Place of Birth, Naming the State, Territory, or Country.	Married within the year	Attended School within the year	(over 20 can't read/write)	Whether deaf and dumb, blind, insane, idiotic, pauper, or convict
1			Coleman S Atwood	21	m		Mariner		Mass				
2			Levi "	18	m		"		"		1		
3			William H "	11	m				"		1		
4			Almira F Rider	9	f				"		1		
5	384	457	Thomas Atwood	51	m		Farmer	400	"				
6			Mercy "	48	f				"				
7			Thomas "	15	m				"		1		
8			Joshua E "	14	f				"		1		
9	385	458	Elisha R Atwood	52	m		Mariner	800	"				
10			Polly "	51	f				"				
11			Mary "	20	f				"				
12			Emily "	18	f				"				
13		459	Elijah Baker	29	m		"		"				
14			Catherine "	26	f				"				
15			Elijah "	5	m				"		1		
16			Joseph E "	3	m				"				
17			Mary E "	1	f				"				
18			Sarah M "	12	f				"		1		
19	386	1460	Richard Atwood	66	m		Farmer	350	"				
20			Cynthia "	64	f				"				
21		461	Uriah A "	68	m		"	300	"				
22			Elisa	39	f				"				
23			Betsy Fielding	53	f				"				
24			Warren "	9	m				"		1		
25			Cordelia "	5	f				"		1		
26			Betsy J "	3	f				"				
27	387	462	Elijah W Atwood	41	m		Mariner	200	"				
28			Grace H "	57	f				"				
29			Cordelia S	16	f				"		1		
30			Samuel A	6	m				"		1		
31	388	463	Joel Atwood	61	m		Carpenter	950	"				
32			Susanna "	63	f				"				
33			Reuben R "	36	m		"		"				
34			Almira "	29	f				"				
35			Ann R "	24	f				"				
36			Joel "	21	m		"		"				
37			Benjamin W "	2	m				"				
38			Barnabas Flanagan	11	m				"		1		
39	389	464	Peter L Atwood	31	m		"		"				
40			Mercy C "	27	f				"				
41			Sylvester B "	6	m				"		1		
42			Henry O "	3	m				"				

SCHEDULE I.—Free Inhabitants in *The town of Wellfleet* in the County of *Barnstable* State *Massachusetts* enumerated by me, on the *7th* day of *August* 1850. *Josiah Gifford*, Ass't Marshal.

1	2	3	4	5	6	7	8	9	10	11	12	13	
Number of the house in the order of visitation	Families numbered in the order of visitation	The Name of every Person whose usual place of abode on the first day of June, 1850, was in this family.	Age	Sex	Color, (white, black, or mulatto.)	Profession, Occupation, or Trade of each Male Person over 15 years of age.	Value of Real Estate owned.	PLACE OF BIRTH. Naming the State, Territory, or Country.	Married within the year.	Attended School within the year.	Persons over 20 y'rs of age who cannot read and write.	Whether deaf and dumb, blind, insane, idiotic, pauper, or convict.	
390	465	Eleazer Atwood	70	m		Seamen	700	Mass.					1
		Semira "	69	f				"					2
		Elliot N "	11	m				"			/		3
391	466	David M King	29	m		Mariner		"					4
		Semmime A "	26	f				"					5
		Catherine O "	1	f				"					6
		Timothy S Atwood	35	m		Painter		"					7
		Anthony "	29	m		Mariner		"					8
392	467	Jesse R "	27	m		"		"					9
		Marian "	25	f				"					10
		Edward B "	6	m				"			/		11
		Anthony "	2	m				"					12
393	468	Israel Pierce	43	m		"		"					13
		Bethiah "	42	f				"					14
		Israel "	22	m		"		"					15
		James F "	19	m		"		"					16
		Benj H J "	19	m				"			/		17
		Warren "	15	m		/		"			/		18
		Alonzo L "	14	m				"					19
		John F "	12	m				"					20
		Deborah R "	9	f				"					21
		Bethiah L "	5	f				"					22
		Wm F "	7	m				"			/		23
		George A "	4	m				"			/		24
		Edward W "	2	m				"					25
		Deborah Ford	48	f				"					26
		Catherine Sweeney	24	f			/	Ireland					27
394	469	Abigail F Higgins	52	f			400	Mass					28
		Thomas H "	18	m		"	100	"					29
	470	Wm Gale	26	m		"		/ England					30
		Abigail "	24	f				/ "					31
		Elizabeth A "	5	f				Mass			/		32
		Otho H "	2	f				"					33
395	491	Daniel L Rich	50	m		Farmer	150	"					34
		Mehitable "	49	f				"					35
		Thatcher "	25	m		Mariner		"					36
		Daniel L "	20	m		Trunkmaker		"					37
		James H "	16	m				"			/		38
		Edwin "	11	m				"			/		39
		Benj "	9	m				"			/		40
396	472	Charley Pape	24	m	blk	Mariner		"					41
		Sarah "	22	f	"			"					42

Bound Brook Island residents end on Line 8 with Sylvanus Rich.

64

SCHEDULE I.—Free Inhabitants in *the town of Wellfleet* in the County of *Barnstable* State of *Massachusetts* enumerated by me, on the *4th* day of *Septem* 1850. *Seabed Gifford* Ass't Marshal

	Dwelling-houses numbered in the order of visitation.	Families numbered in the order of visitation.	The Name of every Person whose usual place of abode on the first day of June, 1850, was in this family.	Age.	Sex.	Color, white, black, or mulatto.	Profession, Occupation, or Trade of each Male Person over 15 years of age.	Value of Real Estate owned.	Place of Birth. Naming the State, Territory, or Country.	Married within the year.	Attended School within the year.	Persons over 20 y'rs of age who cannot read & write	Whether deaf & dumb, blind, insane, idiotic, pauper, or convict.
	1	2	3	4	5	6	7	8	9	10	11	12	13
1	397	473	Nepthalia Rich	50	m		Farmer	1000	Mass				
2			Anna "	47	f				"				
3			Marilla D "	19	f				"				
4			Charles W "	14	m				"		1		
5			Wm T "	11	m				"		1		
6			Sally "	72	f				"				
7	398	474	Rebecca "	56	f			300	"				
8			Sylvanus "	15	m				"		1		
9	399	475	Thomas S "	46	m		Mariner	550	"				
10			Sarah S "	36	f				"				
11			Thankful S "	18	f				"				
12			Drusilla H "	16	f				"		1		
13			Irene S "	10	f				"		1		
14			Pamelia "	2	f				"				
15	400	476	Barnabas Freeman	63	m		Farmer	450	"				
16			Lucy "	64	f				"				
17			Michael "	16	m				"		1		
18			Pousilla R. Lee "	31	f				"				
19			Abigail "	2	f				"				
20			Barnabas "	24	m		Mariner		"				
21	401	477	Wm D Freeman	55	m		"	650	"				
22			Louis H "	43	f				"				
23			Wm D "	22	m		"		"				
24			Allen "	14	m		"		"		1		
25			Hosea B "	12	m		"		"		1		
26			Samuel D "	11	m				"		1		
27			Benj F "	9	m				"		1		
28			Joanna C "	7	f				"		1		
29			Susan L "	5	f				"		1		
30			Wesley J "	3	m				"				
31			Sarah W "	1	f				"				
32	402	478	Elisha Freeman	67	m		Farmer	650	"				
33			Elizabeth "	57	f				"				
34			Rebecca "	30	f				"				
35			David C "	24	m		Mariner		"				
36			Charles Manson "	18	m		"		"				
37			Eben S Earl	12	m				"		1		
38		479	Ruth Reed	65	f				"				
39	403	480	Solomon Rogers	63	m		Farmer	550	"				
40			Sarah "	57	f				"				
41			Abe R "	15	f				"		1		
42			Martha Higgins	76	f				"				

The Liberator, December 1, 1854, masthead and detail from page 3

THE LIBERATOR,
IS PUBLISHED
EVERY FRIDAY MORNING,
AT THE
ANTI-SLAVERY OFFICE, 21 CORNHILL.

ROBERT F. WALLCUT, GENERAL AGENT.

WM. LLOYD GARRISON, EDITOR.

Our Country is the World, our Countrymen are all Mankind.

VOL. XXIV. NO. 48.   BOSTON, FRIDAY, DECEMBER 1, 1854.

Collision of Steamers in Boston Harbor.—

The Ocean steamer for Bath, and the British steamer Canada came in collision near Spectacle Island, in Boston harbor, on Friday evening last. The bow of the Canada penetrated to the express room of the Ocean, and knocked over a stove which was full of fire. The coals were scattered about, kindling flames which almost instantly spread through the boat, and she was burnt to the water's edge. Boats from the Canada, Forest City, Boston, ship Westward Ho, and others, immediately put off to the rescue, and, so far as known, all the passengers, (upwards of 80,) except three who were drowned, were saved. Those lost were a man about thirty, a woman about thirty-five, and a child six. They jumped overboard at the time of the collision. Mr. Hiram L. Wing, Messenger of Carpenter & Co's Express, who was so badly burned, died on Saturday afternoon, at the Massachusetts General Hospital. The Ocean was a side-wheel steamer with wide guards, and in every respect a well-appointed and substantial sea going steamer. She was of 600 or 700 tons burden, about four years old, and owned by Rufus K. Page, of Hallowell, Capt. Nathl. Kimball, of this city, and the owners of the old John Marshall, and cost about $75,000. The Canada had her figure head and bowsprit carried away, and her cutwater and bow somewhat injured. The crew of the Ocean stated that she had camphene aboard, and that the cause of the instantaneous conflagration was the bursting of a large can. Nothing else, save gunpowder itself, could have produced so direct a flame. It is literally impossible that the mere overturning of a stove could set a vessel on fire in double the time of this, without the aid of some extraordinary combustible.

We understand that the Ocean was making her last trip of the season, and it is stated that a portion of her crew taken on board the Canada were in a state of intoxication. They had been on board the Canada but a few moments before they commenced a fight among themselves in the fore saloon. The chief engineer of the Canada rebuked them for such disgraceful conduct under such circumstances.

One lady on board the Ocean, with great presence of mind, seized an egg box, lifted it over the rail of the vessel and threw it overboard, and then with a bound landed on top of it, and paddled about until she was saved by the boats.

Mr. Charles Pope, a colored passenger, who resides at Cape Cod, and follows the fishing business, had his thigh and ribs broken, and it was thought he would not live through the night. His wife was also severely injured. Mrs. Barry, stewardess of the Ocean, was delirious, but was not materially injured.

The light of the fire was seen in this city, and was very brilliant for an hour. Many persons went to the wharves and other localities where the flames were visible. An alarm was given, and the whole fire department went over to South Boston, before the cause of the light was ascertained.

Legend for the 1848 Map

PAGE 71 displays a map of Bound Brook Island. It is a detail from the 1848 "US Coast Guard Survey Map of Cape Cod from Billingsgate to the Pamet River." Below is my guide to the topographical map symbols used by cartographer Henry Whiting.

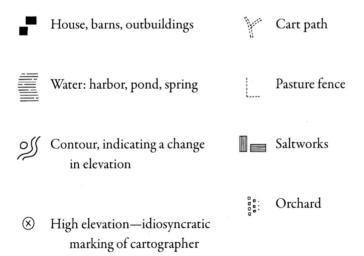

House, barns, outbuildings

Cart path

Water: harbor, pond, spring

Pasture fence

Contour, indicating a change in elevation

Saltworks

Orchard

High elevation—idiosyncratic marking of cartographer

Bibliography

The Acts and Resolves, Public and Private, of the Province of Massachusetts Bay. Boston: Wright & Potter, 1890.

Adams, Mark. *Truro and Beyond: Living on a Changing Coastal Peninsula in the Gulf of Maine.* Cape Cod National Seashore, North Atlantic Coastal Lab, North Truro, Massachusetts, presentation to Truro Historical Society, 2018.

Barnstable County Registry of Deeds, https://www.barnstabledeeds.org

Baylies, Francis. *An Historical Memoir of the Colony of New Plymouth: From the Flight of the Pilgrims into Holland in the Years 1608, to the Union of that Colony With Massachusetts in 1692.* Boston: Wiggin & Lunt, 1866.

Belding, David L. *A Report upon the Alewife Fisheries of Massachusetts.* Boston: Commonwealth of Massachusetts, Department of Conservation, Division of Fisheries and Game, 1920.

Bolster, W. Jeffrey. *The Mortal Sea: Fishing the Atlantic in the Age of Sail.* Cambridge, Massachusetts, and London, England: The Belknap Press of Harvard University Press, 2012.

Braginton-Smith, John, and Duncan Oliver. *Cape Cod Shore Whaling: America's First Whalemen*. Charleston, South Carolina: The History Press, 2008.

Brennessel, Barbara. *The Alewives' Tale: The Life History and Ecology of River Herring in the Northeast*. Amherst and Boston: University of Massachusetts Press, 2014.

Brown, George Goode. *The Fisheries and Fishery Industries of the United States: History and Methods of the Fisheries*, Vol. II. Washington, DC: United States Printing Office, 1887.

Clark, Elmer T. *An Album of Methodist History*. New York: Abingdon-Cokesbury Press, 1952.

Clemensen, A. Berle. *Historic Resource Study: Cape Cod National Seashore, Massachusetts*. Denver Service Center, Historic Preservation Division, National Park Service, Denver: US Dept. of the Interior, 1979. http://npshistory.com/publications/caco/hrs.pdf

Collections of the Massachusetts Historical Society, Vol. VIII. Boston: Monroe & Francis, 1802.

Cronon, William. *Changes in the Land: Indians, Colonists and the Ecology of New England*. New York: Hill and Wang, 2003.

Cumbler, John T. *Cape Cod: An Environmental History of a Fragile Ecosystem*. Amherst and Boston: The University of Massachusetts Press, 2014.

Davis, William Morris. *Geographical Essays*. Ann Arbor: University of Michigan Library, 1909.

Deyo, Simeon L. *A History of Barnstable County, Massachusetts*. New York: H. W. Blake & Co., 1890.

Donaldson, Emily, Lauren H. Laham, and Margie Coffin Brown. *Atwood-Higgins Historic District: Cultural Landscape Report and Outbuildings Historic Structures Report; Cape Cod National Seashore, Wellfleet, Massachusetts*. Boston: National Park Service, Olmstead Center for Landscape Preservation, 2010.

Echevarria, Durand. *A History of Billingsgate*. Wellfleet, Massachusetts: The Wellfleet Historical Society, 1993.

Finch, Robert. *Cape Cod: Its Natural and Cultural History*. Division of Publications, National Park Service, United States Department of the Interior, Washington, DC, 1997.

Freeman, Frederick. *The History of Cape Cod: Annals of the Thirteen Towns of Barnstable County, Vol. II*. Boston: W. H. Piper & Co., 1869.

Freeman, Margaret Zarudny. *Russia and Beyond: One Family's Journey, 1908–1935*. London: Impala, 2006.

Gaines, Jennifer Stone and John York. "Saltworks." *Spritsail: A Journal of the History of Falmouth and Vicinity*, Vol. 21, No. 1. Woods Hole, Massachusetts: Woods Hole Historical Collection, 2007.

Garrison, William Lloyd (ed.). *The Liberator*. Boston, Massachusetts: December 1, 1854.

Gillis, John R. "Cape Cod: An Environmental History of a Fragile Ecosystem." *The American Association of Geographers (AAG) Review of Books*, 4:4, 202-204, 2016. https://doi.org/10.1080/2325548X.2016.1222820

Gosnell, Mariana. *Ice*. New York: Alfred A. Knopf, 2006.

Hall, John H. "Bound Brook Island Revealed," Seth Rolbein (ed.). *A Cape Cod Voice*, February 13–26, 2003.

Herring River Restoration Project: Development for Regional Impact Application. Wellfleet, Massachusetts: Town of Wellfleet, December 2019.

Historic Structure Report: The Atwood-Higgins House, Wellfleet, Massachusetts: Cape Cod National Seashore, 1980.

Hodge, Frederick Webb (ed.). *Handbook of American Indians North of Mexico: N–Z*. Washington, DC: Smithsonian Institution, 1911.

Holmes, Richard D. et al. *Archaeological Reconnaissance Survey of Higgins Hollow*. Cape Cod National Seashore, Truro, Massachusetts. Amherst: University of Massachusetts Archaeological Services, 1985.

Knickerbocker, Wendy. *Bard of the Bethel: The Life and Times of Boston's Father Taylor, 1793–1871*. Newcastle upon Tyne: Cambridge Scholars Publishing, 2014.

Kurlansky, Mark. *Cod: A Biography of the Fish That Changed the World*. New York: Walker and Company, 1997.

Larson, G. J. and B. D. Stone (eds.). *Late Wisconsin Glaciation of New England*. Dubuque, Iowa: Kendall/Hunt, 1982.

Lepore, Jill. *The Name of War: King Philip's War and the Origins of American Identity*. New York: Knopf, 1998.

Lovell, Irving W. *The Story of the Yarmouth Camp Ground and the Methodist Camp Meetings on Cape Cod*. Yarmouth, Massachusetts: privately printed, 1985.

Lowenthal, Larry. *Historic Assessment: Atwood-Higgins Property*. Amherst: University of Massachusetts, 1995.

Macfarlane, Robert, Stanley Donwood, and Dan Richards. *Holloway*. London: Faber and Faber, 2013.

Marr, J. S. and J. T. Cathey. "New Hypothesis for Cause of Epidemic among Native Americans, 1616–1619." *Emerging Infectious Diseases*, 16(2), 281–286. https://doi.org/10.3201/eid1602.090276

McKenzie, Matthew. *Clearing the Coastline: The Nineteenth Century Ecological and Cultural Transformation of Cape Cod*. Hanover, New Hampshire and London: University Press of New England, 2010.

McMahon, Peter and Christine Cipriani. *Cape Cod Modern: Midcentury Architecture and Community on the Outer Cape*. New York: Metropolis Books, 2014.

Morison, Samuel Eliot. *Maritime History of Massachusetts 1783–1860*. Boston and New York: Houghton Mifflin, 1921.

Mourt, George. *A Journal of the Pilgrims at Plymouth: Mourt's Relation*, Dwight B. Heath (ed.). New York: Corinth Books, 1963.

Nelson, Richard. *The Island Within*. San Francisco: North Point Press, 1989.

Newman, Donna. *Geologic History of Cape Cod, Massachusetts*. http://pubs.usgs.gov/gip.capecod/glacial.html

Nye, Everett I. *History of Wellfleet from Early Days to the Present Time*. Hyannis, Massachusetts: F.B. & F.P. Goss, 1920.

Oldale, Robert N. *Cape Cod, Martha's Vineyard & Nantucket: The Geologic Story*. Yarmouth Port, Massachusetts: On Cape Publications, 2001.

Palmer, Albert P. *A Brief History of the Methodist Episcopal Church in Wellfleet, Massachusetts*. Boston: Franklin Press, Rand, Avery & Co., 1877.

Portnoy, John, Alice M. Iacuessa, and Barbara A. Brennessel. *Tidal Water: A History of Wellfleet's Herring River*. Wellfleet, Massachusetts: Friends of Herring River, 2016.

Pratt, Enoch. *A Comprehensive History, Ecclesiastical and Civil, of Eastham, Wellfleet and Orleans from 1644–1844*. Yarmouth, Massachusetts: W.S. Fisher & Co., 1844.

Prins, Harald E. L. and McBride, Bunny. *Asticou's Island Domain: Wabanaki Peoples at Mount Desert Island, 1500–2000*. Boston: National Park Service, United States Department of the Interior Ethnography Program, Northeast Region, Volume 2, 2007.

Private & Special Statutes of the Commonwealth of Massachusetts from May 1830–April 1837. Boston: Dutton & Wentworth, 1837.

Quinn, William P. *The Saltworks of Historic Cape Cod*. Orleans, Massachusetts: Parnassus Imprints, 1993.

Rich, Earle. *More Cape Cod Echoes*. Orleans, Massachusetts: Salt Meadow Publishers, 1978.

Rich, Shebnah. *Truro—Cape Cod or Land Marks and Sea Marks*. Boston: D. Lothrop and Co., 1883.

Schwarzman, Beth. *The Nature of Cape Cod*. Hanover, New Hampshire: University Press of New England, 2002.

St. John de Crevecoeur, J. Hector. *Letter from an American Farmer*. London: Thomas Davies & Lockyer Davis, 1782.

Stark, Mary Lee. *People and Places on the Outer Cape: A Landscape Character Study*. Amherst: University of Massachusetts and National Park Service, 2004.

Strahler, Arthur N. *A Geologist's View of Cape Cod*. Orleans, Massachusetts: Parnassus Imprints, 1988.

Sturgis Library Newspaper Archives, Barnstable, Massachusetts. https://www.sturgislibrary.org/research/notable-collections/newspaper-indexes/

Thirty-Second Annual Report of the Board of Harbor and Land Commissioners, Public Document 11, for the Year 1910. Boston: Wright & Potter Printing Company, 1911.

Thoreau, Henry David. *Cape Cod*. New York: Bramhull House (Clarkson Potter), 1951.

Whalen, Richard F. *Truro: The Story of a Cape Cod Town*. Charleston, South Carolina: History Press, 2007.

Williams, John Taylor. *The Shores of Bohemia: A Cape Cod Story, 1910–1960*. New York: Farrar, Straus and Giroux, 2022.

Willison, George F. *Saints and Strangers: The Story of the Mayflower and the Plymouth Colony*. London: Heinemann, 1966.

Wilson, Charles Morrow. *Dow Baker and the Great Banana Fleet*. Harrisburg, Pennsylvania: Stackpole Books, 1972.

Zion's Herald, 1823–1826, Boston. Microfilm at W. E. B. Du Bois Library, University of Massachusetts, Amherst.

OTHER SOURCES

THS—Truro Historical Society

WHSM—Wellfleet Historical Society & Museum

GCAH—General Commission of Archives and History of the United Methodist Church, Madison, New Jersey

About the Author

SHARON DUNN has published a memoir, *Under a Dark Eye: A Family Story*, and two books of poetry, *Refugees in the Garden* and *My Brother and I*. For 10 years she was editor of the literary magazine *AGNI*. She lives with her husband in western Massachusetts and on Bound Brook Island in Wellfleet, Massachusetts.